Fennings Taylor

Are Legislatures Parliaments?

A Study and Review

Fennings Taylor

Are Legislatures Parliaments?
A Study and Review

ISBN/EAN: 9783337154318

Printed in Europe, USA, Canada, Australia, Japan

Cover: Foto ©Suzi / pixelio.de

More available books at **www.hansebooks.com**

ARE LEGISLATURES PARLIAMENTS ?

A STUDY AND REVIEW.

BY

FENNINGS TAYLOR,

DEPUTY CLERK, AND CLERK ASSISTANT OF THE SENATE OF CANADA,

Author of " Sketches of British-Americans," with Photographs by Notman;
" The Life and Death of the Honourable T. D'Arcy McGee;"
" The Last Three Bishops appointed by the Crown
for the Anglican Church of Canada," &c.

MONTREAL : JOHN LOVELL ; QUEBEC : DAWSON AND CO. ;
TORONTO : G. M. ADAM ; OTTAWA : DURIE AND SON
NEW YORK : JOHN W. LOVELL.
1879.

THIS STUDY AND REVIEW,

BY HIS FRIENDLY PERMISSION, IS CORDIALLY DEDICATED

TO THE RIGHT HONOURABLE

SIR JOHN ALEXANDER MACDONALD, K.C.B., D.C.L.,

&c., &c., &c.,

A STATESMAN

WHOSE LOVE OF LITERATURE AND ART

HAS NOT ONLY PROMPTED HIM EARNESTLY TO MUSE ON

THE WORKS OF

THEOLOGIANS, POETS, ARTISTS, JURISTS AND SATIRISTS ;

BUT WHOSE SYMPATHY WITH

HUMAN NATURE

HAS ENABLED HIM TO FIND REFRESHMENT IN NOVELS

AND

PHILOSOPHY IN ALL WRITINGS WHERE WIT SPARKLES,

OR

WHERE HUMOUR FINDS A TONGUE.

A STATESMAN,

MOREOVER,

WHO HAS GIVEN TO HIS COUNTRY THE FRUITS OF HIS LARGE EXPERIENCE,
RARE INDUSTRY AND MATURE WISDOM, ESPECIALLY ON THOSE
SUBJECTS THAT RELATE TO

PARLIAMENTARY LAW AND CONSTITUTIONAL GOVERNMENT,

AS THEY ARE EXPOUNDED AND ENFORCED BY THE SUPREME AUTHORITY

OF THE

MOTHER COUNTRY.

FOR MY PART I LOOK UPON THE IMPERIAL RIGHTS OF GREAT BRITAIN AND THE PRIVILEGES WHICH THE COLONISTS OUGHT TO ENJOY UNDER THOSE RIGHTS, TO BE JUST THE MOST RECONCILABLE THINGS IN THE WORLD. THE PARLIAMENT OF GREAT BRITAIN IS AT THE HEAD OF HER EXTENSIVE EMPIRE IN TWO CAPACITIES, ONE AS THE LOCAL LEGISLATURE OF THIS ISLAND, PROVIDING FOR ALL THINGS AT HOME IMMEDIATELY, AND BY NO OTHER INSTRUMENT THAN THE EXECUTIVE POWER ; THE OTHER, AND I THINK HER NOBLER CAPACITY, IS WHAT I MAY CALL HER IMPERIAL CHARACTER, IN WHICH, AS FROM THE THRONE OF HEAVEN, SHE SUPERINTENDS ALL THE SEVERAL INFERIOR LEGISLATURES, AND GUIDES AND CONTROLS THEM ALL WITHOUT ANNIHILATING ANY.—*Burke's speech on American Taxation, Vol. I, page 156, of his "Select Works," edited by E. J. Payne, M.A., Fellow of University College, Oxford.*

PREFACE.

—

THE inquiry which has suggested what follows is a very interesting and important one, for it includes a good deal more than a question of grammatical construction, and rises much higher than a mere play on the value of terms that are commonly accepted as interchangeable. There need be no controversy on the etymology of the words in our title page, for their origin and derivation can easily be traced. It may at once be admitted that they are popularly regarded as synonymous and convertible ; nor can their relationship be questioned, for the business of law-making is inseparably interlaced with, and necessarily includes, the duty of talking and consulting. But the question we propose to examine refers less to the ordinary kinship, than to the official use, of the two words " Legislature " and " Parliament." Such examination is the more necessary as the suggested meaning of these words, as supplied by the English statutes, is by no means identical with their common meaning, as given in the English dictionaries. Nor does this divergence exhaust our embarrassment, for the two words have been differently employed, and, consequently, differently interpreted, by the Parliament of the United Kingdom, and by the legislatures of the colonies. Were the distinctions thus drawn only verbal they would scarcely deserve attention. But they are not so. On the contrary, the Imperial Parliament has placed an exact and limited meaning on these initial words, which has either escaped the notice of, or has not been assented to by the provincial legislatures; and, as the distinction made by the former includes some important consequences to the latter, it may be worth while to give the whole subject a patient examination. Indeed, the law of the case can scarcely be interpreted apart from the history of the case, and the latter can only be gathered by a careful reference to the practice of the legislatures, as it is found in the journals and records of the provinces, and these again must be studied with the aid of those lights which actually, or presumably, have been shed on them by ministers of the Crown in England.

ARE LEGISLATURES PARLIAMENTS?

A STUDY AND REVIEW.

―

CHAPTER I.

EXPERTS in the business of drafting acts of Parliament
are generally careful to use the same word whenever,
in the course of their work, they have occasion to refer
to a given subject or to describe a special thing. To
this end an experienced draftsman will avoid synonyms
or equivalents, because synonyms and equivalents cannot be alike in form, and may not be equal in value, to
the words whose places they are employed to take. If,
for example, such an expert means "Legislature" he
would not, when drafting a law, write "Parliament," as
these words, though germane to one another and collo-
quially interchangeable, are separated one from the other
by several well-drawn lines of meaning. Were such an
one, for example, acquainted with the acts passed for
the government of the old provinces, and of the present
dominion, of Canada, he would know that the Parliament of England had been careful to use the words we
have named as terms of contrast, rather than as terms of
resemblance, and, consequently, that they could not be

used indifferently, or interchanged without loss. It is very important to keep in mind the distinction which has thus been drawn for us by the supreme authority, as it is by no means certain that grave mistakes have not arisen, and may yet arise, from a disregard of exactness in determining the " meets and bounds " of the words " Legislature " and "·Parliament." Thus, when we find these words used in an Imperial Act to describe separate powers and separate authorities, we may be sure they are so employed for distinct uses, and are intended to describe, not one, but two political organizations, whose duties, powers and privileges, unless otherwise bestowed, must be sought for in the Act in which they were granted. Being words of grave weight and import, we may expect to find them carefully guarded wherever they are used, and only repeated in the same sense in which they were at first employed. The advantage of such a practice is obvious, for the occasions for doubting about the relevancy of language are lessened, and the work of interpretation is rendered comparatively easy. The commentator is relieved of the duty of assaying the weight, or of adjusting the value, of terms that may be similar but that are no alike ; that may spring from kindred germs, and yet display marks more or less pronounced of divergence, if not of contrast, in their development. Such marks as are commonly observed between the looseness of conventional and the precision of legal phrases.

For the convenience of illustration, and by way of
preface to the subject of this work, reference will be
made to three acts of the Imperial Parliament and to
the words employed when describing those political
institutions, which colonists, from early association, and
probably from a foregone interpretation, have regarded
as " Parliaments," but which the mother country intended to be " Assemblies," or " Legislatures " and
nothing more.   The first example will be found in the
Act 31st George 3rd, which authorized the separation of
the province of Quebec into Upper and Lower Canada,
wherein provision was made for the establishment
" within each of the said provinces respectively of a
Legislative Council and an Assembly."   It is to be
noted that the word " Legislature " is nowhere used
in that act as an alternative expression, much less as
an equivalent one for the word " Parliament," nor is the
word " Parliament " used, even remotely, as a term
applicable to the experiment then initiated of a new
model of colonial government.

In like manner, in the Act of 3d and 4th Victoria, 1840,
which re-united the then separated provinces of Upper
and Lower Canada, the like exactness in the use of
words is strictly observed.   " There shall be within the
province of Canada one Legislative Council and one
Assembly," " which shall be called the Legislative Council and Assembly of Canada," is the language of the
act, for the word " Parliament " is nowhere applied to

the legislature created by that act.   Indeed, as we
shall have occasion to observe presently, the word
" Parliament," as applied to the legislature of Canada,
with all " the powers, privileges and immunities " which
that majestic and historic term seems to have been formed
to express, was employed for no common use ; but, like
a cherished dignity of the highest order, was reserved for
a later occasion and for a larger, a more imposing and
expressive purpose."   It will be observed that the powers
conferred by the two acts to which we have referred
were enabling and co-operative powers.   They were " to
aid His (or Her) Majesty, by and with the advice and
consent of the Legislative Council and Assembly, to
make laws for the peace, welfare and good government
of the inhabitants of the respective Provinces."

The machinery by which such work was to be done
was generally, rather than specially, described in what we
are accustomed to call the constitutional acts.   The aim
was clearly stated, but the means seem to have been
left to their intelligence who should be chosen to put
the machine in motion.   The right to make laws for the
good government of the province included the authority
to make rules for the good government of the legislatures.   But such rules were to be subordinate to law,
for the colonial Assemblies had neither inherited, or
had conferred on them any freedoms, exemptions or
advantages that were inconsistent with or superior to
the law.   No " powers," no " privileges," no " immuni-

ties " beyond the law-making power were given to the law makers. On the contrary, while those acts contained several disqualifying and disabling clauses they did not include one on which a special privilege could be fastened, or under which a personal immunity could be claimed. The Acts of 1791 and 1840, which thus authorized the establishment of Councils and Assemblies within the provinces of Canada, apparently were passed to enable certain persons chosen, or elected, for the purpose, to aid their Sovereign in making laws, that, under express limitations, were to be operative within, and not beyond, the boundaries of the respective provinces. The functions of such legislatures, as originally bestowed, if for convenience we may be allowed a diminutive form of expression, were municipal in their range, and the laws of such legislatures, like those of less imposing corporations, were only operative within, and not beyond the municipality, no matter whether such municipality was termed a district or a province. The duties originally discharged by such legislatures, though certainly more imposing and extensive, were scarcely more final and complete than are those which are now performed by county and city corporations. In either case the power exercised was of a statutory character. Every act passed was declared to be passed in virtue of the authority conferred by a higher legislature, *i. e.*, the Parliament of England. Everything done by the Legislative Council and Assembly was done in virtue of the

law which created such council and assembly, and of
that only. It follows that as authority, like water, can rise
no higher than its source, we may look only to the law to
which those assemblies owed their existence as their
warrant and justification for such things as they did, and
for such immunities as they claimed. "Custom and
usage" were exotics, and hence the common law could
not properly be appealed to where the case to be
dealt with was to be found only within the limits of a
modern statute. Analogy afforded no help, for law and
not "use" controlled the law makers.

The Canadian Assemblies, moreover, were experi-
ments. One province was a thinly settled country with a
newly organized government, and both provinces were to
be made the scenes of new modes of administration. The
hoar of age, the sanctity of tradition, and the hereditary
influence being absent from, or not yet naturalized in, the
new country, could have no place in the new Legislatures,
and consequently "usage and custom," which derive
from use and age, must have been absent also. Until the
passing of the British North America Act of 1867 it
may fairly be questioned whether a comparison could
reasonably have been made between the statutory Councils and Assemblies of the British colonies in America
and the Parliament of England. The phrase "image
and transcript of the British Constitution" was a phrase
of singular but exaggerated felicity. which nevertheless
reflected most truly the feeling and desire of the enthu-

siastic and chivalrous Governor Simcoe. Unfortunately the charm of the phrase must be sought for in the regions of feeling and desire, of imagination and fancy, as it will be looked for in vain in the sober limits of a law which included no individual privileges, conferred no personal immunities and preserved no ancient customs, but which had come as fresh from the brain of the British Parliament as the coin that on the same day may have issued from the English mint. No doubt Governor Simcoe's picturesque words fell smoothly on the sympathetic ears of the loyalists to whom they were addressed, for they were laden with soothing euphony. They touched alike the hearts, the imaginations and the histories of all the Upper Canadians of that day. As an epigram daintily compounded of feeling and flattery, it quickened their spirit, and sank into their mind, while in later times it was caressed and fondled, remembered and quoted with satisfaction and excusable pride. Nor was such a result surprising. For however far removed the newly created legislature that first met at Newark, now Niagara, in 1792, was from the "ancient inquest of the English nation," it was highly agreeable, no doubt, for "Honourable Gentlemen and Gentlemen" who were members of that legislature to be informed by an authority so distinguished as the representative of Majesty, that the estates of the province of Upper Canada, there gathered within the four walls of the Legislative Council chamber, was a "Parliament," the image and transcript of that glorious constitution for which those loyal legislators had been willing to fight, and were ready to die ; for that constitution whose origin they knew, or had been told, was to be sought for in the remotest times ; the image and transcript of those grand estates whose early history they believed was to be found, not in the written law, but in " the deep trod footprints of ancient custom."

The Acts of 1791 and 1840 were conventionally and properly called " Constitutional Acts." And whatever legislative authority was exercised within the provinces was so exercised in virtue of the authority which those acts conferred. The laws passed by the councils and assemblies established by those acts, when assented to and left to their operation by the Parliament of England, were valid within the province in which they were passed ; just as the laws of the local legislatures, when assented to and left to their operation by the Parliament of Canada, are now valid within the province in which they are passed. But the " privileges, immunities and powers" which from time immemorial had been held, exercised and enjoyed by the Parliament of England, and which by the terms of the " British North America Act " are " now held, exercised and enjoyed " by the Parliament of Canada, are not named in the acts of 1791 and 1840, nor are they alluded to in the debates and explanations that arose during the passing of those acts. It would therefore seem that the Imperial Parliament most carefully and with great exactness weighed the language of its laws ; for the qualifications and conditions which in the acts of 1791 and 1840 seem to hedge the legislatures established by those acts, are repeated in 1867 and applied to the legislatures that were, or might thereafter be, established under the British North America Act. It would therefore seem that the British North America Act of 1867 may be regarded as the interpreter of the two previous acts, for it not only uses the words " Parliament " and " Legislature," but for the first time it defines alike their meaning and their powers. Indeed the discrimination is so broad that none can fail to understand the scope and relevancy of the two words. Both the " Parliament of Canada " and the " Provincial Legislatures " are the creations of the same Act, but the former, with the name and the title deeds, has been invested with the customs and privileges of ages, while the latter has succeeded only to such rights, duties and powers as the act itself specifies and confers. The British North America Act of 1867, in thus discriminating between words which in Canada have practically been treated as synonymous, pointedly suggests for our consideration a by no means unimportant fact, viz. : that as a " Legislature " is a body distinguished from and not identical with a " Parliament," so must it be ruled by the conditions of its creation, and not by the conditions under which the body from which it is distinguished was created. A " Parliament " possesses hereditary as well as inherent rights. A Legislature possesses only charter rights ; for it has no other or higher powers than those contained in the act under which it is established, and therefore its authority, like the authority of a municipality, is absolutely limited by the law. If then this inference be just, it would seem to follow as an absolute conclusion that the "privileges, immunities and powers" claimed and exercised by the members of the old legislatures of British North America, and by the members of the different legislatures of Canada at the present time, were, and are, so claimed and so exercised without warrant or authority of the Parliament of England.

This mortifying discovery very naturally gives rise to an interesting question. If the Imperial authorities did not intend the legislatures which they created to exercise the functions of Parliaments, then, after what other pattern were they formed, and with what inquests lower than Parliaments may they be compared? Is it possible that, when providing the means of local self-government for the different provinces of North America the Imperial Parliament was more guided by the system of rule which obtained in Saxon England than by the grander and more imposing one that arose after the Norman conquest? For, although the former system was overridden and trampled down, so far as it affected the country at large, it nevertheless survived in certain forms, and still lives in a more or less modified condition, in every municipality in England. May not the ancient corporation of the city of London, for example, with its two orders of aldermen and councilmen, its limited area and charter rights, have suggested the form of local self-government, which was subsequently adopted, with respect to the two Canadas. The councillors and assemblymen of the legislatures, whether appointed or elected, like the aldermen and councilmen of a municipality, are taken from the democracy, and the limit of authority in either case is determined by exact boundaries, no matter whether they be civic or provincial. But, without dwelling unduly on this inference, there can, we think, be only one conclusion arrived at from the evidence which the three constitutional acts furnish of the aim and intention of the Imperial Parliament in passing those acts. We are no longer left to guess the meaning of the acts of 1791 and 1840, neither have we the right any longer to assume that they conferred powers that were not expressed. The British North America Act of 1867 not only interprets itself but furnishes the key by which we are to interpret its predecessors. The last named for the first time gives authority to create outside of the United Kingdom a Parliament whose members shall have such privileges, immunities and powers " as are held, enjoyed and exercised by the Commons House of Parliament of the United Kingdom of Great Britain and Ireland and by the members thereof." As no such "privileges, immunities and powers " were conferred on any of the legislatures established by the three acts we have mentioned, and as they are by contrast actually with-

held from the legislatures that are established by the
last mentioned Act, it follows conclusively that the
assumption in the past, or at the present time, by Provincial legislatures of the "privileges, immunities and
powers " that belong only to Parliaments is an assumption for which no authority can be found in the acts
under which those legislatures were established, and
from whence all their authority is derived.

If, however, the intention of the Parliament of England
was absolutely plain, the action of the legislatures of the
two Provinces of Canada was still more expressive.
While only swaddled in swathing bands those sturdy
infants did not hesitate to cover themselves with the
clothing of Britannia, or to claim, like their counterpart,
the Parliament of England, that they also were " the heirs
of the ages," the inheritors of the usages of a thousand
years.   Hence they lost no time in appropriating " privileges " that had not been conferred, in claiming " immunities " that had not been bestowed, and in exercising
" powers " that had not been granted.   The transaction
was a charming compound of innocence and audacity.
Nevertheless the " privileges, immunities and powers,"
though boldly asked for and adroitly appropriated, as if
they had been the unquestionable accessories and attributes of legislative government, were not enjoyed without
a challenge.   There were some who doubted, and there
were others who denied, that an Assembly was a Parliament.   They questioned the right to claim, under cover

of privilege, powers and exemptions that had no place in the law. But their scepticism was scouted by the legislature, and was not then carried into court, and so it came to pass that customs which had been appropriated without warrant were continued without law. And here a question of a qualifying character very naturally arises. As the " privileges, immunities and powers " so ostentatiously bestowed by the first Governor of Upper Canada, and more cautiously by the first Governor of Lower Canada, and their successors, were not so bestowed in virtue of any power authorized by law, it follows that if authority can be produced for the exercise of such powers it must be sought for elsewhere than in acts of Parliament. Is it to be discovered in the Colonial office? or can it be found in the form of Royal instructions? Were the law officers of the Crown consulted, and, if so, where are we to look for their opinions? The point could hardly have been settled off-hand, for it included the two attributes of privilege and prerogative. Now a privilege, or an immunity, is commonly understood to be an exception to a law, while a prerogative, though a legal function, is a function above the law. This exception to law was claimed by Speakers of successive Assemblies, and was allowed by successive Governors. Thus a function above the law was exercised by successive Governors, and presumably by the authority that was delegated to them, but of which we fail to discover any evidence. It follows that successive

Governors, in virtue of this actual or supposed authority, arrested the course of law, by stepping between debtors and creditors, to the serious loss and injury of the latter. In like manner, successive Governors set themselves above the law, and incidentally at all events, in virtue of the privileges conferred, gave authority to the legislatures to attach and imprison whom they would, without reference to the courts ; and yet Governors and Speakers alike escaped open rebuke or pecuniary loss. No indemnity was sought for the exercise of what we think must now be considered to have been acts of questionable legality. Privilege and prerogative embraced one another, and results of a very irritating kind were the issue of the compact. " Privileges, immunities and powers," which we now know are the exclusive property of Parliaments, were seized and enjoyed by Assemblies that were not intended to be Parliaments. The appropriation, it must be allowed, was open and above board, and whether right or wrong, whether legal or illegal, the privileges, so far as words could convey them, were as fully given as they were frankly asked for. Governor Simcoe did not wait to balance phrases. He probably thought that as a Parliament was a Legislature it followed that a Legislature was also a Parliament, and consequently he looked upon the infant Legislature of Upper Canada as an infant Parliament. Again, he had enjoyed the advantage of sitting in the Parliament of Great Britain as a member for a Cornish borough, and consequently he was in all probability familiar with the forms and usages of the House of Commons. He had possibly been present at the election of a Speaker, and was therefore aware of the customs observed at such imposing ceremonials. In the new departure, when inaugurating a typical representative government for colonial use in Upper Canada and elsewhere, he would no doubt have been especially anxious to make a good beginning. He would remember the ancient rights and undoubted privileges that were asked for and granted in England ; and reasoning from the analogies he had constructed, and fitted in his own mind, he would naturally conclude that the like privileges ought to be extended to, even if they were not inherent in, the members of the Legislature of Upper Canada. He did not pause to ask whether he could exercise a prerogative which he did not possess, or whether, without authority, he could bestow privileges which were to supersede the operation of law. It must of course be presumed that the members of the new Assemblies had reason to believe that their petition for privileges would be favourably received, and it must also be assumed that the Governors had, or thought they had, authority to grant what was asked for.

Nevertheless, from the circumstances that attended the election of the first Speaker of the Assembly of Upper Canada, and to which more particular allusion will hereafter be made, it is probable that this doubt was not wholly absent from the mind of Governor Simcoe, as an unusual delay occurred between the election of the Speaker and the customary prayer for privileges. But whatever may have been his doubts, Governor Simcoe apparently had arrived at the conclusion that no difference within their respective limits existed between the Imperial Parliament and the Local Legislature, and consequently it was His Excellency's pleasure to look on the latter as the " image and transcript" of the former. But it must be borne in mind that no license to observe a system of constitutional analogy was either directed or required by the constitutional act of 1791. And hence, in order to justify the bestowal on the newest Assembly in America of the "privileges, immunities and powers " of the oldest Parliament in Europe, it was necessary, in His Excellency's opinion, by an act of personal authority, to assent to a certain mode of procedure which should have the effect of grafting ancient custom on modern law, and of clothing with the privileges of ages the legislative experiment that was born on that day.

We have no knowledge that Governor Simcoe had any authority whatever for thus placing himself above the law, and it is very doubtful whether such authority could have been conferred by Royal instructions even had the attempt been made. Consequently we must assume that no such instructions were issued, for no evidence of their existence can be found. The act was a personal one, and took its rise in the error which was corrected seventy-five years afterwards by no less an authority than

the Imperial Parliament, viz. : that two legislatures that
were dissimilar in name, and unequal in their attributes,
were likewise the reverse of identical in the inherent
rights they severally possessed, and in the privileges and immunities they respectively enjoyed. It
is probable that His Excellency's mind was undisturbed
by doubt, and consequently that he made no effort to
discover a difference between two disproportionate
bodies that exercised unequal functions and were called
by different names. Having, as he believed, in virtue
of his prerogative, declared the lesser to be the image
and transcript of the larger body, he established between
the two a claim to identity, and was content to leave his
opinions, and his epigram, to work like leaven in the
Canadian mind, until at length few persons were found
to question the soundness of the former while none
denied the felicity of the latter. Nevertheless, if our in-
ferences and conclusions are correct, we now learn that
Governor Simcoe's opinion was unsound, and the language
in which it was clothed inexact and misleading, for the
Imperial Parliament has corrected both by publishing its
own interpretation of its own words. After seventy-five
years in one case and twenty-six in the other of erroneous
practice, the meaning of the constitutional Acts of 1791
and 1840 is explained by no lower authority than the law
maker, who informs all whom it may concern that a
" Legislature " is not a " Parliament," and consequently
that the " powers, privileges and immunities " which have

been and still are exercised by Legislative Councils and
Assemblies are nothing else than fond conceits, com
menced without authority and continued without warrant.
The error is easily explained. Apparently it took its
rise in inexactness and a loose interpretation of words.
But the mistake has run its course, and it is now corrected. We learn on the supreme authority of the Parliament of the United Kingdom that the words " Legislature"
and " Parliament," which were commonly regarded in
Canada as synonyms, are scarcely more equivalent in
their meanings than they are alike in their forms. The
illusion is dispelled. But it was not cherished, as there
is reason for believing, without criticism, at the Colonial
office, or without challenge in Canada. There were
some in the Upper Province who denied that a " Legislature "was a " Parliament," and being consistent, for they
were so to their cost, they asserted that the Assemblies
arrogated powers that had not been granted to them, that
they instituted comparisons that could not be drawn, and
so arrived at conclusions that ought not to be reached.

We shall defer our further criticism and the narrative
that has given rise to it, till a later chapter. In the meanwhile it may be observed that, as history generally
sparkles with contradictions, so it need occasion no
surprise if the events of past days in Canada now and
then find expression in paradox. The political conduct
of one generation will not always be found consistent
with the received opinions of the next. They were the re-

formers, for example, who grafted Parliamentary government on the Provincial legislatures, but they were the tories who, firmly believing that the written constitution of Upper Canada was the " image and transcript" of the unwritten one of England, firmly set their teeth at all gainsayers, and especially at those who sought to dwarf the dignity of their legislature by questioning whether it had, or ought to have, the powers, privileges and immunities of Parliament. The late Mr. Robert Baldwin, the late Mr. James Small and others succeeded even before the time had properly arrived, and notwithstanding the opposition of the tories, in clothing the legislatures with the attributes of Parliament, while the fathers of those gentlemen, viz. : the Honourable William Warren Baldwin, better known as Dr. Baldwin and Mr John Small failed, notwithstanding the veiled sympathy of reformers, in their efforts to minimize local authority and individual importance, by asserting, and by acting on their belief, that the Legislature was not a Parliament, and, consequently, that the members thereof had no legal right or title to the immunities they claimed or the privileges they appropriated.

The story is curious, and at the time occasioned a good deal of commotion in " the town of York." Dr. Baldwin and Mr. Small were salaried officers of the government. Standing on what they believed to be their rights, they denied that " Assemblies " were " Parliaments," and, consequently, that members of the former could legally avail themselves of the shelter of privilege, as privilege was the especial and peculiar property of members of the latter. They went further, for, having the courage of their convictions, they provoked a test case by causing a member of the Assembly to be arrested for debt. A lively scene arose. The Legislative Council and Assembly, for a wonder, were thoroughly in accord, so they joined hands and entered into an offensive and defensive alliance. Of course the members of the Assembly lashed themselves into a vehement rage, which naturally articulated itself in the rhetoric of the gutter, for weak politicians generally use strong words, and Assemblies with limited powers usually indulge in unlimited talk. The reason was not far to seek. The members of those deeply agitated Houses were by no means satisfied with their own securities, for they had thought themselves to be the undisputed owners of more valuables than they actually possessed. It was surmised that they had mistaken pinchbeck for gold, and had possibly circulated counterfeit for real coin. Being threatened with forfeiture and loss, they displayed great tenacity in clinging to what they had appropriated. Wherefore they determined to stamp out heresy on the spot, and to this end used their heaviest words and their hardest measures. They not only passed violent resolutions, but followed them by acts of high-handed oppression. Dr. Baldwin, being the greater offender, was dismissed, without a hearing, from his place, while Mr. Small saved himself from deprivation by making an humble but skilful apology.

CHAPTER II.

EXACTITUDE in the use of terms, as we have already insisted on, is an important aid to every branch of study, but it is especially so in matters of science. Controversies would often be avoided were we to agree beforehand on the meaning and the measure of the words to be employed, and fix with precision their relative as well as their actual value. In fact, a problem is said to be half solved when the terms in which it is to be stated are previously settled. The science of government, for example, depends very much on the systematic arrangement of formulas, and the course of law is also hedged in with set phrases, whose meanings have been established by usage and precedent. The truth is that in all matters of serious concern great attention should be paid to terms, and great caution observed in the use of supposed equivalents; for a correct understanding of an instruction, and more especially of a law, may depend on the condition whether the same things have uniformly been described in the same words.

These observations bear very directly on the case under review. Canadians of the last century substituted a gloss for the text of an Imperial Act, and their suc-

cessors, for two or three generations, moved by considerations of example and convenience, continued the practice, until at length time and use have done much to
crystalize error and give it the semblance of truth.
But in tracing a wrong practice to its source we must
leave the responsibility where it should rest, viz. : with
the authors.   They were the founders of our constitution, and   notably Governor Simcoe and the early
legislators of Upper Canada who made the first slip,
and thus glided, innocently no doubt, and honestly we
are quite sure, into the mistakes of practice which Dr.
Baldwin challenged, and which the Imperial Parliament,
fifty-five years later, endeavoured by law to amend and
correct.   Let us bear constantly in mind that the
word Parliament as an equivalent for Legislature is
neither to be found in the text nor in the marginal notes
of the Act of 1791, nor is it to be found in the text, but
as if by an oversight, it has crept into two of the
marginal notes of the Act of 1840.   Dr. Baldwin's contention was that a Legislature was not a Parliament, and,
had he lived a quarter of a century longer than he did
live, he would have had his opinion sustained by the
concurrent testimony of the Houses of Lords and Commons, for "The British North America Act 1867"
expressly declares there shall be one Parliament for
Canada, and one Legislature for each of the several
provinces.

The " Parliament for Canada " shall consist " of the

Queen, an Upper House, styled the Senate, and the House of Commons."

There were also to be legislatures for the different provinces, consisting in each case of the Lieutenant Governor and of one House, or of two Houses, as might be deemed advisable.

The constitution of the supreme Parliament for Canada is in marked contrast with the constitution of the subordinate legislatures. Indeed the framework differs as much as the phraseology. "The image and transcript of the British constitution," which is repeated and preserved in the Parliament of Canada, becomes a fiction and disappears altogether when we seek to apply it to the legislatures of the provinces. The legislatures not only differ in their constitution from the Parliament, but they differ from one another. The Sovereign is not expressly included in their component parts, nor is it necessary that those parts should be three in number. In fact, Ontario started with only two estates, and other Provinces have followed, while others seem inclined to follow the example of Ontario. Thus as strong an emphasis as language can articulate is placed on the fact that the two bodies so created were distinct and distinguishable one from the other, for, while there can be no doubt that a Parliament is a Legislature, we have the authority of law for saying that a Legislature is not a Parliament. Furthermore, after explaining in what way the Parliament of Canada shall be constituted, the Act, as if to

clear away all ambiguity, adds in the next clause that
the "powers, immunities and privileges to be held,
enjoyed, and exercised by the members thereof respectively shall be equal to, but shall not exceed, those at
the passing of this Act held, enjoyed and exercised by
the Commons House of Parliament of the United Kingdom of Great Britain and Ireland and by the members
thereof." The Imperial Parliament in 1867, as it previously had done in 1840 and in 1791, defines also,
and be it observed in contradistinction to the previous
definition of a Parliament, in what way the Provincial
Legislatures are to be constituted and carried on. The
two definitions are fairly rounded and seem thoroughly
complete. Positively we are taught by the words of the
statute what legislatures are ; and negatively we learn
by the eloquence of silence what legislatures are not.
The conclusion appears to be irresistible. They are not,
and consequently never could have been, intended to be
Parliaments ; for they are not in the latest, nor were they
in the acts under which they were at first incorporated
penetrated with those quickening, animating and distinguishing " privileges, immunities and powers " which
are emphatically declared to be the exclusive and especial
possession of the Parliament of the United Kingdom,
and of the Parliament of Canada and of the members
thereof respectively.

It may, however, be advisable to refer to " The British
North America Act 1867 " and quote what it says. Un-

der the head " Legislative Power " the Act declares
in the seventeenth clause, " there shall be one Parliament for Canada, consisting of the Queen, an Upper
House styled the Senate, and the House of Commons."
The clause following enacts that " the privileges, immunities and powers to be held, enjoyed and exercised by
the Senate and by the House of Commons, and by the
members thereof respectively, shall be such as are from
time to time defined by any Act of the Parliament of
Canada, but so that the same shall never exceed those at
the passing of this Act held, enjoyed and exercised by
the Commons House of Parliament of the United Kingdom of Great Britain and Ireland and by the members
thereof."

" The Parliament of Canada Act of 1875 " enlarged
the last mentioned clause and made it more comprehensive. The amendment runs thus. After " Canada,"
where it is last mentioned in the above quotation, the remaining words are left out and the following substituted :
" but so that any Act of the Parliament of Canada defining such privileges, immunities and powers shall not
confer any privileges, immunities or powers exceeding
those at the passing of such Act are held, enjoyed, and
exercised by the Commons House of Parliament of the
United Kingdom of Great Britain and Ireland and by
the members thereof."

Whatever the privileges that are " held, exercised
and enjoyed " by the members of the English House of

Commons may be, whether they have their roots in acts of Parliament or in ancient custom, whether they existed " before the time of memory," or rest on the common law, no matter whence or how derived, those " privileges, immunities and powers," neither more nor less, have been gathered, consolidated and in the set form of law extended to and conferred on the members of the Senate and House of Commons of Canada. It is thus evident that the Imperial Parliament was of opinion that the " privileges, immunities and powers " which they enjoyed, whether inherited or acquired, were vested in themselves alone, and could only be delegated to another legislature within the British Dominions by a positive act of their own, an act moreover that should be authenticated with all the forms and solemnities of Parliament. In the absence of such a positive act, and the opportunity of passing one had often arisen, it would seem to follow that the assumption of powers that had not been conferred, like the assumption of titles that had never been bestowed, was neither more nor less than a fond conceit, wrought, it may have chanced, from the tissue of analogy and sentiment, but not from the harder strands of law and authority.

Until the passing of " The British North America Act, 1867," no legislature within the colonial dominions of Great Britain had been established to compare with the Imperial Parliament, and hence when colonial Assemblies, with excusable complacency,

sought to clothe themselves with powers which had
not been conferred on them, or when they claimed
the privileges of a body whose name even they did not
bear, the proceeding was probably overlooked, or if
noticed, the authors were possibly regarded as harmless
trespassers on a manor that was not theirs, and perhaps
excused because such assumptions could injure no one
beyond their own borders.   It should nevertheless be
borne in mind that the Parliament of the United Kingdom neither directly, or otherwise, concurred with the
legislatures of British North America in the opinions
which the latter had formed on their " privileges,
immunities and powers," for had it done so there would
have been no need to pass a new law, no need, by a
special act, to confer immunities that were already assumed, to bestow privileges that were already possessed,
or to grant powers that were already enjoyed.   The
seventeenth and eighteenth clauses of the British North
America Act were new features in colonial charters which
expressed real meanings and not idle words.   They gave
authority for doing what, so far as we can discover, had
previously been done without authority.   They made
that legal and right which before was illegal and wrong.
They removed doubts, for doubts had existed; they
quieted controversy, for controversy had arisen; and
while they neither condoned nor reviewed the past, they
made the course of future conduct clear.   Indeed, had the
eighteenth section been left out of the Act few would now

c

question the propriety of continuing a practice which was
begun in inadvertence, but which had been locally sanc-
tioned by use.   Originally Governor Simcoe's epigram
though felicitous was misleading, and must we think be
regarded as an exaggerated, and to a grave extent a
misapplied expression of opinion, which led to an
exaggerated and unlawful exercise of authority.   But the
like exercise of authority was repeated by successive Governors and by successive Speakers.   Indeed, no successful
resistance appears to have been made to the practice,
and consequently no abatement of the authority assumed
took place for many years.   The forms and procedure
were honestly continued after the fashion which Governor
Simcoe had set, nor were they modified, as we shall
have occasion to show, without causing what appears
to have been a somewhat violent wrench.   In the meanwhile a precedent of eighteen years duration was established in Lower Canada, and of a longer period in Upper
Canada ; and precedents, we all know, usually bear fruit.
In the words of Junius, "what was yesterday a fact to-
day is a doctrine ; what was yesterday a precedent to
be challenged, to-day is a law to be obeyed." If the Act
of 1867 had not said a new thing, and said it emphatically ;
if it had been as silent on the points on which it has
spoken as were the two preceding acts, we should have
assumed that the prerogative which had theretofore been
exercised was still exercisable, and that the "privileges,
immunities and powers" which had theretofore been

enjoyed were still enjoyable, and consequently that the sixty-fifth clause which ratifies all that was lawfully done before 1867 would have ratified, for example, what was done by successive Governors when they placed their authority above the law and shielded debtors from arrest ; and what was done by successive Assemblies, when in the absence of prescriptive right they peremptorily hailed offenders to attend at their bar, and exposed them to the penalties of a tribunal which, without law or delegated authority, peremptorily assumed the right to arrest, to try, to fine, and to imprison. Thus does "the British North America Act of 1867" teach us that Governor Simcoe, and many besides, who lived in " the good old times," and since then, seriously exaggerated the "beneficence" of the mother country, and drew only a caricature when they meant to make a portrait of the " image and transcript of the British constitution," for it was evidently no part of the Imperial plan to do more than to plant the English colonies with Assemblies whose duties and powers should be limited by law. Their Constitutions were to be, and were written ones, and the acts in which they were embodied, from beginning to end, in the text and in the intention excluded the very name of Parliament, and consequently excluded the conditions that grow out of that name, viz. : Parliamentary privileges and Parliamentary government, albeit the former were retained in obedience to a passionate act of assumption, while the latter were acquired by the courageous exercise of endeavour. In the former case the law was possibly warped for personal ends, while in the latter it was undoubtedly enlarged for the public good.

It has frequently been said that England was never without national assemblies of some kind or other. Mr. E. A. Freeman writes that "the germs alike of the monarchic, the aristocratic and the democratic branches of our constitution will be found as far back as history or tradition throws any light on the institutions of our race." Thus it may have been that the early settlers of North America, in imitation of the constitution of the British Parliament, and notably in the colony of Virginia, were apt, of their own mere motion, to distribute the governing power, when they were not interrupted in doing so, in three parts. The first was lodged in the Governor, the second in a Council of State and the third in an Assembly composed of representatives freely chosen by the people. In referring to the colony of Virginia and to the first representative body, if we mistake not, that ever assembled in America, we may add that it was just such a body of select men as the English race on sudden emergencies is apt to call into action. For, though it was organized under the direction of a private company, it was for all practical purposes nothing less than a self-constituted domestic legislature, chosen for the purpose of regulating the general affairs of the country. The experiment proved so acceptable to the people generally that, in 1621, the ruling council of the company in

England went a step further. Without the shadow of
authority, they issued an ordinance which gave the new
form of government a permanent sanction and with
more extended powers. This action on the part of the
company, being an act of independent and unauthor-
ized legislation, offended King James; for it was
contrary to his opinions, and formed no part of his practice, to put the royal authority into commission. Wherefore that monarch took a peremptory way of stopping
colonial imitations of English originals. The company
quailed under the King's displeasure, and retreated
hastily within their former lines, while matters of administration at once reverted to the condition in which they
were before the issue of the objectionable ordinance.
But, had the King's prerogative been also seized and
exercised without his consent, such a liberty, being
viewed as a personal affront, would no doubt have been
visited with a punishment more severe than a frown.
Those adventurous colonists and others who followed
their example in establishing legislatures by and with
the advice and consent of trading companies, or of their
own mere motion, were thereafter careful to guard
themselves on this point. They did not claim to possess,
nor did they attempt to use, the privileges of members of
the House of Commons. The time for doing so had not
arrived. Nevertheless after the revolution, and probably in imitation of the Parliament of Great Britain
such privileges and exemptions, to a qualified extent,

were extended to the Congress of the United States, and were enjoyed alike by senators and by members of the House of Representatives. The evidence of this fact will be found in the 6th sub-section of the first article of the Constitution of the United States wherein it is declared that "Senators and Representatives shall in all cases, except treason, felony and breach of the peace, be privileged from arrest during their attendance at the session of their respective Houses, and in going to and returning from the same," and "for any speech or debate in either house they shall not be questioned in any other place."

It may now be interesting to turn to the early chapters of our Canadian histories and see by the entries in the earliest Journals of Upper and of Lower Canada, how such privileges came to be acquired and the circumstances that attended their bestowal. By the Act of 1791 it was declared that the Legislature of Upper Canada should consist of a Legislative Council of seven members and of a House of Assembly of sixteen members. The first Journal of the Legislative Council opens thus:

"Newark, Monday, 17th September, 1792.

Prayers were read by the REV. MR. STEWART.

PRESENT:

The Honourable	RICHARD CARTWRIGHT, jr.
WILLIAM OSGOODE,	JOHN MUNRO,
JAMES BABY,	ALEXANDER GRANT,
ROBERT HAMILTON,	PETER RUSSELL.

The house was a full one, for all the members were in attendance. Then the Honourable William Osgoode, who was also the Chief Justice of Upper Canada, produced his commission, and was sworn in as Speaker of the Legislative Council.

The Journals of the House of Assembly of the same day inform us that all the members having met, and being sworn in by William Jarvis, Esq., unanimously elected John MacDonell, Esq., one of the members of the county of Glengarry to be their Speaker. The name is suggestive, for doubtless it belonged to one of that race whom fortune has favoured, for subsequent history informs us that it has won a foremost place among the governing families of Upper Canada. The election of the Speaker having been made, the House of Assembly, in obedience to the command of His Excellency Governor Simcoe, attended at the bar of the Legislative Council.

Thus, according to Governor Simcoe's view of the occasion, were the three estates of the Upper Canada Legislature, consisting of twenty-four persons, assembled to make laws " for the peace, welfare and good government" of the province. They met at the small town of Newark, now Niagara, being the temporary capital, where some military works had been erected. Whether the building wherein the infant legislature first assembled is now standing we know not, but, as the town has since then been made familiar with adventure and vicissitude, it is probable that this interesting historical me-

morial is lost alike to sight and to memory. The Council chamber in all probability was a small room, but
the ceremony must have been somewhat imposing, while
the speech, which crowned all, is grand enough for the
most elaborate building and the largest audience. After
this manner His Excellency the Lieutenant-Governor,
John Graves Simcoe, addressed both Houses :

" Honourable Gentlemen of the Legislative Council,
and Gentlemen of the House of Assembly.

" I have summoned you together under the authority of
an Act of the Parliament of Great Britain, passed in the
last year, and which has established the British Constitution, and also the forms which secure and maintain it in
this distant country.

" The wisdom and beneficence of our Most Gracious
Sovereign and the British Parliament have been eminent-
ly proved, not only in imparting to us the same form of
government, but also in securing the benefit by the many
provisions that guard this memorable Act, so that the
blessings of our invaluable constitution, thus protected
and amplified, we may hope may be extended to the
remotest posterity.

" The great and momentous trusts and duties which
have been committed to the representatives of this
Province in a degree infinitely beyond whatever till this
period have distinguished any other colony, have origi-
nated from the British nation upon a just consideration
of the energy and hazard with which the inhabitants

of this Province have so conspicuously supported and defended the British Constitution.

" It is from the same patriotism now called upon to exercise with due deliberation and foresight the various offices of the civil administration that your fellow subjects of the British Empire expect the foundation of that union of industry and wealth, of commerce and power, which may last through all succeeding ages. The natural advantages of the Province of Upper Canada are inferior to none on this side of the Atlantic : there can be no separate interest through its whole extent: the British form of Government has prepared the way for its speedy colonization, and I trust that your fostering care will improve the favourable situation, and that a numerous and agricultural people will speedily take possession of a soil and climate which, under the British laws, and the munificence with which His Majesty has granted the lands of the Crown, offers such superior advantages to all who shall live under its government."

The seven gentlemen who composed the Legislative Council and the sixteen gentlemen who composed the House of Assembly must have felt a good deal elated by the speech to which they had listened, for it certainly encouraged them to magnify their office and to think a good deal of the positions to which they had been preferred, and of the distinctions that had overtaken them. Nor were they without reasons for self-complacency and legitimate pride. In their collective capacity, whether

Municipal, Legislative or Parliamentary, they were the founders and forerunners of those representative governments which thereafter should be called into existence in the colonies of England, and established also after the pattern furnished by the Canadian Legislatures.   More than this, the modest gathering at Newark represented the germ of an imposing future.   Those seven Legislative Councillors and sixteen Assembly men very aptly prefigured what came to pass seventy-five years later, when the germ opened and blossomed into the Parliament of Canada, and the shanty hall at Newark into the grandest pile of Gothic architecture on the continent of North America.

The immediate effect of the opening ceremony showed itself somewhat differently in the two branches of the Legislature.   The members of the Upper House appeared to have seen their way clearly as they proceeded at once with the business of the session.   The members of the Lower House, on the other hand, apparently needed more time to steady themselves.   They hesitated as if seized with the thought that what they had done had been done imperfectly, for on returning to their chamber a motion was immediately made to adjourn, and the house was accordingly adjourned till the following day.

The first entry on the journals of Tuesday, 18th September, 1792, seems to have been intended to repair an irregularity, for it sheds some light on the summary termination of the previous day's sitting. Some one, probably the Governor, who, for reasons already stated, was no doubt conversant with the forms of the Imperial Parliament, discovered on the very threshold of the proceedings what he regarded as an important omission, as well as a marked difference in the ceremonies observed between choosing a Speaker at Westminster and at Newark ; a difference which His Excellency no doubt thought on this important initial occasion should at once be removed, as it represented a serious blot on the " image and transcript of the British constitution " which His Excellency so dearly cherished and caressed. An error in substance as well as in form evidently was supposed to have occurred, as the Speaker whom the Assembly had elected had not been presented for His Excellency's official approval. This, no doubt, was not only regarded as a lack of respect, for the early settlers rarely failed when compliments were due to the Crown, but as an oversight of serious constitutional importance. It was considered to mean a good deal more than a mere question of the approval of the person chosen as the Speaker, for it included such matters as the liberty of speech, the right to offer counsel, and above all freedom from arrest. As soon, therefore, as the house met the next day the following entry occurs :

"On motion made and seconded, it was ordered, That Mr. White and Mr. Jones wait upon His Excellency to know when he will be pleased to receive the House, that the Speaker may be presented for his approbation."

Later in the day those gentlemen " reported that His Excellency will receive the House immediately."

" The House waited upon His Excellency accordingly."

" The Speaker reported that His Excellency had been pleased to approve of the Speaker chosen by the House, and to promise that the Members of the House shall enjoy freedom of debate, access to the person of His Excellency, and be privileged from arrest."

The privileges of the British Parliament were thus, nominally at least, and in exact terms, accorded to a colonial Assembly. The claim to privileges seems to have occurred to the latter in the manner of an after thought. We are not informed in what words it was made, but it was evidently granted by the Governor without hesitancy, as if he had no doubt of his right to do so. But where the authority is to be looked for, since it cannot be found in the constitutional Act of 1791, or in the Governor's commission, or in the Royal instructions, which are regarded as explanatory of both, are questions more easily asked than answered.

On Monday, the 15th October, 1792, after " prayers and a sermon " His Excellency went to the Council chamber and required the attendance of the House of Assembly ; after assenting to several bills His Excellency closed his interesting speech with the following suggestive sentence : " Honourable Gentlemen and Gentlemen, I cannot dismiss you without earnestly desiring you to promote, by precept and example, among your respective counties the regular habits of piety and morality, the surest foundations of all public and private felicity, and at this juncture I particularly recommend to you to explain that this Province is singularly blessed not with a mutilated Constitution but with a Constitution which has stood the test of experience, and is the very image and transcript of that of Great Britain, by which she has long established and secured to her subjects as much freedom and happiness as it is possible to be enjoyed under the subordination necessary to civilized society."

Upper Canadians, with good reason, have always revered the character and cherished the memory of their first Lieutenant Governor. It is easy to see in reading his two speeches what manner of man he was, for the spirit of enthusiasm that glistens in his words is of that ennobling quality that quickens slower minds and raises inferior natures to higher and purer levels. Had it been his lot to open the first Parliament, instead of the first Legislature, of Canada, he would have approached the duty in the spirit of lofty exultation, and, from the warmth of his heart and the exuberance of his fancy would have spoken words of congratulation, encouragement and hope. There would have been no allusion to another confederation or to a fancied utopia ; there would have been no hint of a rent in the British commonwealth, no suggestion of a new departure for the English-speaking race. Governor Simcoe's longings were Imperial, and, no

doubt, were tempered with the opinions that governed
the statesmen of his age. It would have been impossible
for him to have harboured a thought, much less to have
breathed a word, on the subject of a " new nationality,"
for such a thought would have represented a baffled mission and such a word would have meant a broken Empire.   The grace to inspire enthusiasm is not bestowed
alike on all, and they can but ill convey the gift whose
nerveless breasts are haunted with quailing fancies and
shivering fears.   Governor Simcoe did not gauge the
popular sentiment by a process of arithmetic, or determine the worth of national will by a discipline of figures.
Such labours were foreign alike to his habits and his
tastes.   Duty and courage were his watchwords, and to
fulfil the former and display the latter were the natural
expressions of his true and loyal heart.   Consequently his
name and memory have always been, and still are, regarded as precious possessions by the descendants of
the first settlers of Upper Canada.

At the close of His Excellency's speech " The
Speaker of the Honourable Executive Council " (*sic*) declared by His Excellency's command both Houses to be
prorogued to Monday, the thirty-first of December next.

The form adopted no doubt savours of the usage of
Parliament, as, by an exercise of the prerogative, for
which no provision had been made, the life of the two
Houses was apparently continued, and, it may be added,
for a period nearly twice as long as was then customary

in England or as is now the practice in Canada. With respect to "the Parliament of Canada" the formula observed at Westminster may properly be used, for it has the authority of law, but whether it can with equal propriety be employed by subordinate Legislatures, may reasonably be doubted, as there is no evidence that such a technical continuity was ever intended to be given to any of those Provincial Assemblies that were established before 1867 or to those that are now established under the British North America Act of 1867.

Again, the occasion of the prorogation of the first session of the Upper Canada Legislature supplies what seems like a new example of inexactness, for the words Legislative Council and Executive Council are frequently used as interchangeable terms. In those early days, however, the duties of the two bodies were practically united, and Legislative Councillors were probably *ex officio* members of the Executive Council. Nevertheless, as the Government for many years was a personal one, it is also probable that very little resort was had to Executive advisers, for the Governors of that period affected to seek counsel only when they required it, and that was very seldom. The excuse for such indeterminate language is probably to be found in the fact that a select Council to correspond with the Privy Council was necessary, in the opinion of Governor Simcoe, to perfect in Upper Canada the image of the British Constitution which had become impressed on his mind. Hence the

Legislative Council was called upon to support a dual
character, as it has since done in other North American
colonies, and to bear a double name.   It was an advis-
atory body to the Governor and a Council of assistance
and restraint to the House of Assembly, and there is
little doubt the nominal arrangement was acceptable to
His Excellency, chiefly because the three-fold expression
of colonial rule presented a not wholly inexact correspondence in his opinion with the three parts of the
British Constitution.

The form of the new Government was an experiment,
and, but for Governor Simcoe's stimulating rhetoric, it
would probably have been carried out on Municipal
rather than on Parliamentary lines; for the interpretation
furnished by the British North America Act of 1867 leads
to no other conclusion than that a much less ambitious
organization was intended than the one which His
Excellency's creative fancy called into existence, and
which his poetic temperament stimulated by a too free
use of analogies—of analogies that were but hazily
examined before they were actually applied.   Instead of
being indefinite and antique, the accredited offspring
of remote custom and ancient use, the powers bestowed
were exact and modern, experimental and newly born.
They were charter powers only whose nature and extent
were to be found, not in the transmitted usages of
ages, but in the modern Act out of which they took
their rise.   The two Houses of the Legislature, like

clubs, or guilds, or friendly societies could no doubt make rules and orders for their own discipline and guidance, but such rules and orders would have been, and would be, inoperative were they opposed to, or subversive of, the supreme law.

It follows, then, that, should the Legislatures thus established have found their work hindered or their usefulness impaired by reason of their lacking certain incidents or attributes of authority which the law did not bestow; should they have needed " privileges, immunities and powers" beyond those which the law had conferred, it would have been their clear duty to seek what was lacking at the source of supply and ask the law makers to amend their own work. That they did not do so must be attributed to the fact that the neces. sity for doing so had not arisen, or having arisen had peremptorily been adjudged as inapplicable and dismissed as inoperative, for, whether by right or by usurpation, they exercised to the full the privileges, the immunities and the powers of Parliament. Being in possession, so to speak, whether disputed or otherwise, it was more adroit to avoid explanations than to make them, to assume a good deal and to say nothing. Consequently it was highly impolitic to ask ugly questions, or inquire too closely by what authority such advantages were claimed and such things were done. But policy, as an extinguisher, generally wears itself out. The light it is intended to suppress commonly destroys it, and sooner or

later the truth is revealed.   Thus it was on the occasion
under review.   Dormant issues were revived, and a
question that might have been looked upon as settled
and foreclosed was, by the British North America Act
of 1867, so thoroughly re-opened that it has again to be
faced, again to be inquired into, and again to be determined.

Judging from the course that Governor Simcoe took,
the inference follows that His Excellency was of opinion
that the representative of the Sovereign, like the Sovereign, derived his authority in all unprovided cases
from ancient custom and from the common law, so
that whatever the King could do in the British Islands,
his representative could do in a British Province.   He
seemed to think that the attributes of the Sovereign
belonged also to the representative of the Sovereign, and
that the rights of the Crown attached to, and could *ex-
officio* be exercised by, the representative of the Crown.
Moreover, successive Governors and successive Assemblies appear very generally to have been of the same
way of thinking.   It may therefore be of advantage to
look closely into the matter, and see to what extent and
in what form the Crown devolved its authority, and then
inquire whether authority can legally be taken that is not
to be found in such form.   We cannot logically admit
two sets of propositions that contradict one another.
We are forced to recognize facts that are self-evident,
even though by doing so we should be obliged to resist

conclusions that imply the negative of such facts. What then are the facts? The representative of the Sovereign exercises his delegated powers either because such powers are functions inherent in his office, or because he has been invested with them by the mandate of the Sovereign. That they are not functions inherent in the office of representative of the Sovereign is made clear by the fact that a Governor is an Imperial minister, and his functions consequently are limited and guarded by the articles of his service. No doubt he is the representative of his Sovereign, but like other representatives of their Sovereign, such as judges, sheriffs, and the minor officers of the courts, his representation is limited by law, by the terms of an Imperial act, by the restrictions of his commission, and by Royal instructions explanatory of both. Apart from duties of police and defence, which usually attach to the office of all Governors, and for the exercise of which a wide discretion is allowed, there remain very few questions that are not wholly controlled by what are conventionally called constitutional acts, but which might also be described as local charters. The powers themselves and the mode of exercising them will generally be found in the instruments to which reference has been made. There is small space either for vain conceit or for rash assumption, for the orders and directions are stated generally with clearness. The limits of authority are well laid down, and the inference to be drawn is that the representative of the

Sovereign is to act within his instructions and according to law, and not beyond them. In an important particular there is a special delegation of a royal attribute, in the absence of which the Sovereign would be exposed to the danger of grave misrepresentation. As the fountain of mercy, for example, means had to be found for exercising the prerogative of mercy. The Crown, under certain conditions and within certain restrictions, has conferred on its representative this function of grace. He may pardon criminals, mitigate penalties and remit fines. Thus were offences against the Crown brought within the clemency of the Crown, and being matters of criminal law they stand within the range of royal cognizance. But no such powers were, or could be, delegated in matters of civil process. The King could not by the exercise of a personal act command his representative to interpose between debtors and creditors, and save the former from arrest by the latter. He could not authorize his representative to raise Houses of Assembly into courts of justice, because the act under which they were established had placed exact limits to their powers, such limits indeed as excluded the notion of indefinite expansion. Silence on these subjects in the law, in the commission and in the Royal instructions must be accepted as exclusive, for we learn as plainly in such passages of silence what was withheld, as by the documentary evidence we read what was granted.

Indeed the powers conferred on Governors were generally tentative and rarely absolute. The words of the Royal instructions may easily have been made to apply to other matters than acts of the legislature, for they seem especially, though not expressly, to point to functions of the Governor. They run thus : " And we do further enjoin you not to propose any act whereby our prerogative might be diminished or in any respect infringed without our special permission previously obtained." That the acts of the Governor were not also included in the instruction respecting acts of the Legislature is probably to be ascribed to the fact that the Crown could not have anticipated that a Royal function would have been appropriated and used by its representatives without asking and obtaining the Royal permission to do so. But not only were certain laws not to be proposed but some were not to be assented to, and others were to be reserved for the signification of the Royal pleasure, while those which received the Governor's sanction were liable to be disallowed by the Imperial Parliament at any time after they had been proclaimed in Canada. Even in the matter of patronage and official appointments, the Governors walked in fetters. No Legislative Councillor, no Judge, no important functionary could be appointed without reference to the Colonial office. Neither were such references mere matters of form, for it sometimes happened that the Governor's recommendations were overruled by the Minister. Again, should the representative of the Crown be called on to exercise vice-regal functions, such as conferring titles of honour, a special dispensation from the Sovereign was deemed necessary to the discharge of the special duty.   In fact all extraordinary exercises of authority were absolutely forbidden. To confer " powers, immunities and privileges " not authorized by law was an extraordinary exercise of authority, and should have been regarded as absolutely forbidden.   If small encroachments on the rights of the Crown were to be resisted, larger ones were to be condemned.   The conclusion appears inevitable.

Thus it would seem that Governor Simcoe made a serious mistake when, in the absence of law and authority, he used the King's name without leave to do what the King personally was powerless to perform, for His Majesty could not screen debtors from their creditors.   In the absence of law the King could not authorize the arrest, imprisonment and fine of offenders by such self-constituted courts as Legislative Assemblies, any more than he could do so under the authority of such statutory corporations as County Councils.   Neither could he by any exercise of personal authority confer on such Assemblies privileges to which they were not entitled by law, which Governors were powerless to bestow, and which the Sovereign and Parliament of England evidently did not intend that they should possess.

CHAPTER III.

ABOUT two months after the first session of the Legislature of Upper Canada had been closed at Newark, the first session of the Legislature of Lower Canada was opened at Quebec, but the initiatory proceedings in the two provinces were more remarkable for their divergence than for their similarity. The forms which are observed by the English House of Commons at the beginning of a Parliament were overlooked or misunderstood by the House of Assembly of the upper province. They may perhaps, in the first instance, have been considered inapplicable when we bear in mind that the provincial electorate did not exceed in number the population of one of the smaller county towns of England. being estimated at about ten thousand persons. But no such embarrassments accompanied the initiatory proceedings in Lower Canada, for in that province English precedents apparently had been as earnestly initiated by the members of the Assembly as they were cleverly avoided by His Excellency the Lieutenant-Governor. The customs and usages of the Parliament of Great Britain, together with the exceptional advantages which those phrases were understood to express, were assumed, equally with the

powers conferred by the constitutional Act, to be the inherited and indefeasible properties of the Provincial
Legislatures.   There seems to have been no difficulty as
to the principle, but a doubt appears to have arisen as to
the question of degree.   Some hesitated, as if afraid
to appropriate on no other authority than questionable
analogy, the privileges of another representative body,
whose origin and history was wholly dissimilar to the
one of which they found themselves members.   Hesi-
tation was succeeded by compromise, which found
expression in elaborate motions, long debates, and suggestive divisions, debates that were not even exhausted
when, after much expenditure of time and thought,
the discussions appear to have been brought to an
abrupt and unsatisfactory close, perhaps by the impa-
tience of the Lieutenant Governor, but at all events by
the arrival of Black Rod.   Indeed, the order of procedure in the two Provinces was strangely contrasted.
In Upper Canada the forms observed by the English
House of Commons were not in the first instance followed, and this fact encourages the suspicion that they were
either unknown, or regarded as out of place, by those who
afterwards took advantage of them by making the Provincial ceremonial conform to the Imperial pattern.
Governor Simcoe, as we have already surmised, in all probability suggested what he thought was wanting, and in
this way the missing link was supplied on the day following the one on which the speech was delivered.   More-

over, it seems to have been done with little consideration and less debate. The result was that the humble were exalted, for the Upper Canadian representatives, having failed at the right time to ask for any immunities, were spontaneously rewarded at the wrong time with a grant of all the privileges they could desire, including some which, as we venture to think, they had no reason to expect, and which His Excellency the Lieutenant Governor had no right to bestow.

The concessions which had been so boldly made at Newark were more cautiously considered at Quebec, for the example of Lieutenant Governor Simcoe was rather avoided than followed by the Lieutenant Governor of Lower Canada, Major General Alured Clarke, afterwards Sir Alured Clarke. Indeed the difference of procedure was so marked that the thought arises whether it was due to maturer counsels, to a more careful reading of the law to a severer view of duty, or to some timely caution on the important subjects of authority and competency. In the presence of the facts we shall presently state, it is difficult to dismiss the belief that observations in some influential quarter had been made on the question of privileges between the time when the opening ceremonies of the Upper Canada legislature were observed, and the time when those of Lower Canada were being considered. Unlike the Upper Canadian representatives, who avoided debate and forgot to petition, the representatives of Lower Canada invited discussion and boldly claimed for the provincial representatives all the immunities which the members of the English House of Commons enjoyed. The enumerated privileges may have caused the Lieutenant Governor to reflect, for they were comprehensive enough to provoke hesitancy, to subdue rashness, and to make him call a halt seriously to inquire where such pretentions were to be found. That His Excellency did something of the kind seems evident from the narrative of what subsequently took place, for while the Speaker, on behalf of the Assembly, demanded for its members special privileges, the Lieutenant Governor, on behalf of the Crown, promised only lawful ones.

The occurrences of the 17th December, 1792, and those of the two following days were very interesting. Since the conquest of England, when Saxons, Danes and Normans united in blending as in treble strands the traditions of their races, and thus gradually developing what eventually became the Parliament of the English people, no such Legislative partnership of international members had been attempted as that which was formed at Quebec on the 17th December, 1792. Wolfe and Montcalm, victor and vanquished, each in a shroud of glory, but in distant graves, lay peacefully at rest, but the recollection of the decisive battle which transferred half a continent to Great Britain was well remembered, not only in England and France, but by the elders of that period resident in Canada. Time, we may conjecture, had scarcely sufficed to cool the blood, much less to heal the scars

that war had wrought. Reconciliation to the new rule
could only be looked for as a later condition, and as the
result of justice and kindness on their parts who should
be called on to represent the new sovereignty. Time and
space were alike needed to effect their perfect work.
Nevertheless, what seemed so unpromising actually
occurred. The enmities of opposing races were not only
appeased but they were exchanged for friendliness and
peace. The experiment which Saxons, Danes and Normans had successfully made centuries earlier was again
to be attempted. Under other names the descendants of
the same peoples co-operated for the like ends and with
the like results. The natural enemies of one another, as
the English and the French had been popularly .
regarded, became friends, each according to his light,
and both under a solemn oath, swearing by God's help
to work together for their common country and for the
common good. The scene must have been an impres-
sive one, for the poetry of it still lingers in the fancy, and
it would be well were the historical parallel studied and
worked to completion, for it is generally an act of wisdom
to imitate what experience has pronounced very good.
And what is that parallel? Though remembering with
pride the races from which they sprung, the Saxon, the
Dane and the Norman were content to lay aside their
cherished names, and mutually to submit to a new
baptism in the presence of such sponsors as patriotism
and peace. And by the new name they thereafter be-

came known through all ages as Englishmen. So also might the English and French races in British North America, even while cherishing the memory of their ancestors, and prizing, as each has the right to do, their heritage of fame, be well content to interlace their historic rivalries with their historic laurels, and thereafter to appropriate to themselves the name of the country in which they were born or in which they dwell, and, without hesitancy or resort to qualifying adjectives, call themselves " Canadians ". Nor does the parallel end here. As the " councils " or " inquests " of the Normans, the Danes and the Saxons eventually merged into and became the Parliament of England, so also did the Legislatures of British North America, composed, though not equally, of English and French members, eventually become the Parliament of Canada. In both countries the " grand inquest " enjoys the advantage of having sturdy relations. In England, beside the High Court of Parliament, there will be found a group of time-honoured municipalities and ancient guilds which have gathered wisdom, accumulated wealth, preserved customs, practised hospitality, bestowed honours and dispensed charity ; which have guarded property, protected life and suppressed crime ; which have also promoted health, built highways and lighted streets ; which have housed the houseless, fed the hungry, sheltered the sick, and educated the ignorant ; which in times of peace have pursued their way in quietness and confidence, but in times of war have proved towers of strength to and imposing outworks of the Great Parliament of England. No doubt many of these municipalities and guilds have their party colourings, as well as their political bias, but such considerations have been and are generally subordinated to the ends for which the institutions were created, viz. : the amelioration and improvement of localities and the happiness and benefit of individuals.

Neither is moral aid wanting to the Parliament of Canada. Like her English prototype, she has federal as well as municipal supporters, and these again under different names, but with similar organizations, labour by kindred plans towards common ends. It is the duty of the municipalities of Great Britain and of the municipalities of Canada, irrespective of their names or of their territorial extent, to care for localities, to advance improvement and generally to promote peace, order and contentment. But besides these common obligations, the municipalities of the mother country, in some instances are the repositories of especial privileges which by reason of their antiquity as well as of their value they have shown a praiseworthy anxiety to cherish and protect. In like manner the local legislatures possess local authority and civil rights, which they enjoy under the guarantee of a statute of the United Kingdom ; but in both cases, we venture to think, the possession rests on the authority of law, or on the guarantee of treaty, and not on usage merely, much less on constructive assumption. Such

privileges, when menaced, have been asserted in the past,
and such rights, if interfered with, would be insisted on
in the future. .Less than forty years ago the corporation
of London successfully resisted the Parliament of the
United Kingdom when it attempted, without having
obtained the consent of that ancient guild, to interfere
with the police arrangements of the municipality ; and so
in like manner would the local legislatures spring to their
feet were any effort made by the Parliament of Canada
to curtail their lawful rights, or abridge the powers they
have received from the Parliament of the United Kingdom. It is not of course to be expected, and perhaps not
to be wished, that a body of public men should have
colourless opinions on political subjects, as such a condition is scarcely consistent with a healthy representative
system, or with the nature of men who have been educated
and brought up in the habits of such a system. But on the
other hand it is very much to be desired that politics
should not control subjects with which they ought to
have no connection and to which they do not properly
belong. The heat requisite to the full development of a
colour may often be oppressive, and is sometimes unbear-
able, but it may nevertheless be necessary for the purpose for which it is employed. On the other hand, the influence of "burning questions," being too frequently
forced upon and blended with the discussion of every-day
subjects, not only frets the speakers and warps the argument, but hampers the discharge of duty by hindering,

and rendering acrid, the efforts of honest endeavour. The result is usually deplorable, for where questions that are reasonable and local are controlled by passion and foreign considerations the chances are that faction will triumph while justice will hide herself for shame.

To return to our narrative. As in our last chapter we made an abstract from the earliest journal of the Assembly of Upper Canada, so in this one we shall supply a like abstract from the first journals of the legislature of Lower Canada. On Monday, the 17th December, 1792, the legislature of Lower Canada was assembled for the first time, Major General Sir Alured Clarke being the Lieutenant Governor. The Legislative Council was composed of fifteen members and the House of Assembly of fifty members. The names of the Legislative Councillors present were as follow:

The Honourables

WILLIAM SMITH, *Chief Justice of the Province, and also Speaker of the House.*

HUGH FINLAY.	JOSEPH DE LONGUEUIL.
PICOTTE DE BELLESTRE.	CHARLES DE LANAUDIERE.
THOMAS DUNN.	GEORGE POWNALL.
EDWARD HARRISON.	R. A. DE BOUCHERVILLE.
FRANÇOIS BABY.	JOHN FRASER.
JOHN COLLINS.	HENRY CALDWELL.
J. G. CHAUSSEGROS DE LERY.	

For some reason, not apparent on the face of the writs, they seem to have been thus recorded by the Clerk of the Crown in Chancery: " Writ of Summons to the Upper House of Assembly or Legislative Council.

(Signed), " FINLAY, C. C. in ch."

By referring to the constitutional act of 1791, as well as to the debates thereon in the Imperial Parliament, it will be noted that a much greater amount of care was observed in creating the Upper, than in forming the Lower, Houses in the two Provinces. Legislative Councillors were not only to be nominated for life, but, in the discretion of the home government, provision was made for the formation of a hereditary aristocracy. These considerations should not be lost sight of, for they suggest the thought that, as more precaution was observed in constituting the Upper, than the Lower Houses, so was it the intention, at least at first, to lean more on the nominated, than on the representative bodies of the constitution for the good government of the respective provinces.

It is also to be observed that the style used in the journals of the Legislative Council and of the Legislative Assembly in describing the first meeting of the two Houses is different. In this respect the Upper House seems to have taken the grand attitude, for in their proceedings they use the language of the Lords and not the language of the statute. The words employed in the journals of the former body are :

"At the Provincial Parliament begun and holden at Quebec, in pursuance of an Act passed in the Parliament of Great Britain." Then the title of the Act of 1791 is quoted, but that act, as has already been stated, created a Provincial Legislature and not a Provincial Parliament. The House of Assembly in in their journals, on the contrary, made no mention of the word Parliament, but were content to be guided by the Imperial statute, and thus called itself a "House of Assembly."

The incidents connected with the election of the first Speaker of the House of Assembly of Lower Canada are alike interesting and suggestive. In a House of forty-six, out of fifty Members, Mr. Jean Antoine Panet, the grandfather of the present Deputy Minister of Militia, was elected Speaker by a majority of ten votes.

Three days afterwards, the following entries occur, and as they relate to privileges, we shall quote at length:

Thursday, 20th December, 1792.

"Mr. Speaker elect having taken the chair proposed as questions to the House, and on which he wished to take advice of the House (to wit),

"That the Speaker, being presented at the bar, he should say:

"I humbly pray Your Excellency to consider that I cannot express myself but in the primitive language of my native country, and to accept the translation in English of what I have the honour to say."

E

" The translation to be read by a Member of the House."

" My incapacity being as evident, as my zeal is ardent, to see that so important a duty as that of the first Speaker of the Commons House of Assembly of the Representatives of Lower Canada be fulfilled, I most respectfully implore the excuse and command of Your Excellency in the name of our Sovereign Lord the King."

" If the election of the Speaker is approved of he may say,

" I most humbly claim, in the name of the same Assembly, the freedom of speech, and generally all the like privileges and liberties as are enjoyed by the Commons of Great Britain, our Mother Country.

" That the proceedings of the Representatives may receive the most favourable construction, and that whatever the Speaker shall say may be imputed to his ignorance and not to the Commons, that he may resort again to their House for declaration of their true intent, and that his error may be pardoned."

Lastly, " That, as often as necessary for His Majesty's service and that the good of the commonwealth shall require he may, by direction of the House of Commons, have access to the person of His Excellency the Governor of the Province."

Whereupon Mr. Grant moved the following Resolution, viz: " That when Mr. Speaker elect shall be approved by His Excellency the Lieutenant Governor, he do imme-

diately thereafter, by humble verbal petition to His
Excellency in the name and on the behalf of this Commons House of Assembly, lay claim to the like rights
and privileges as the Commons of Great Britain in Parliament exercise, hold and enjoy, particularly that the
persons of the members of the Assembly, their estates
and servants may be free from arrests and all molesta-
tions ; that the members may enjoy liberty of speech in
all their debates, may have access to His Excellency's
person whenever occasion shall require, and that all
their proceedings may receive from His Excellency the
most favourable construction ; that whenever Mr. Speaker
speaks that may be taken in evil part, may be imputed
to his ignorance and not to the Commons.

" An important amendment was made to the above
resolution by which the words ' servants and estates ' were
left out, but on the question being put whether the resolution as amended should pass, it was resolved in the negative by a majority of twelve votes."

"Then M. P. L. Panet moved, that the Speaker do
demand from the Governor the rights and privileges of
this House as amply as they are enjoyed by the House
of Commons of Great Britain."

Mr. Panet's amendment seems not to have been put
to the House ; though, from what took place afterwards
in the Legislative Council, it evidently expressed the
sense of the House of Assembly. Apparently the whole
proceeding was interrupted by the appearance of Black

Rod, who, in His Excellency's name, commanded the members to attend him in the Legislative Council House (*sic*), with their Speaker.

We may accompany the Lower to the Upper House. After an apology for addressing His Excellency "in the primitive language of his native country" and some confessions of humility, Mr. Panet said :

"I most humbly claim in the name of the House of "Assembly the freedom of speech, and generally all the "privileges and liberties that are enjoyed by the Com-"mons of Great Britain our Mother Country."

To this His Excellency answered, and it must be confessed with discreet vagueness :

"The House may depend on being allowed the full exercise and enjoyment of all just rights and lawful privileges."

His Excellency's speeches at the opening and closing of the Session, though not wanting in congratulatory words, were much more guarded in the opinions they expressed on the constitutional powers of the provincial legislatures than were the speeches of Governor Simcoe on the like subjects in Upper Canada. The privileges conceded to the members of the two Assemblies, whatever they may have been, were such only as could lawfully be given, for they possessed no other value than the value they derived from the law. Hence the most generous, open-handed Governor, could only bestow what he possessed, and if such possessions were not to be found in, and authorized by the law, the gift, whatever it may have seemed, was in point of fact nothing worth. Thus the privileges so honestly asked for and so ostentatiously bestowed, when fairly examined, will be found so meagre, not to say worthless, as scarcely to be distinguished from a blank cheque. The ceremonial dialogue when stripped of its effusiveness, and being withdrawn from the pageant to which it was indebted for any merit it had, represents only a collection of well chosen vapourish words. Being paraphrased they mean this and nothing more : " That the Governor, as an act of duty to his Sovereign and of courtesy to the people whom he had been appointed to rule, will grant their representative free access to his person on all seasonable occasions. They will also as a matter of right, and irrespective of His Excellency's will, continue to enjoy all the rights of British subjects under the common law, together with any special advantages which they may be able to claim under the constitutional Act of 1791." " The privileges, immunities and powers " of Parliament had been asked for, no doubt, but they had not been granted by any one having competent authority to make such a gift. They had been seized and appropriated, and for seventy odd years enjoyed, but they were not actually bestowed until 1867, nor even then were the Provincial Legislatures the beneficiaries of such exceptional gifts. Hence it follows that whatever was done in the earlier days, and whatever may be done

in the present time in virtue of such seizures, or
under such pretences, was and is done without the sanction of law by which those Legislatures are created, and
with only the shadow of insufficient authority.

The first session of the legislature of Lower Canada was brought to a close on the 9th May, 1793, when,
after finishing his speech, the Lieutenant Governor said :
"I do in His Majesty's name prorogue this General
Assembly to Monday the seventeenth day of June next,
and the same is prorogued accordingly." It thus appears
that the claim to privileges was put forward in a somewhat tentative way. In the Upper Province the application reads like an afterthought. In the Lower Province
it appears clear that the majority of the House of Assembly thought it safer to ask for general than for particular powers. The answer, moreover, is the reverse of
encouraging, for the Assembly was informed that they
should continue to exercise and enjoy what they undoubtedly possessed, viz. : their just rights under the common law, and any lawful privileges they could find in the
constitutional act ; for neither of which was any special
permission needed.

It sometimes happens that names or designations
assumed for convenience, or in deference to a personal
wish, or to the claims of euphony, and remaining
unchallenged, in the lapse of time are accepted as
matters of right, and as beyond the range of cavil
or dispute. For example the Legislative Council of

Lower Canada, without the slightest authority that we have been able to find, beyond what the etymology of the word affords, began their first days of journal by styling the two Houses of their Assembly " The Provincial Parliament." This was the commencement of a course of self-appropriated advantages. To associate valuable things with valuable names was natural enough, but it led to the error of not distinguishing between things that were not the same, and were intended by the supreme authority to be different. Moreover the word Parliament especially commended itself to the French mind, for it came of Gallic parentage. It was pleasant to hear, and convenient to repeat, so it was soon adopted by the Canadian and other colonial legislatures. No doubt the title was assumed in good faith, for it was the common belief then, as it has continued to be with the majority of people since, that the words " Parliament" and " Legislature " were synonyms, and meant one and the same thing. But this belief, though general enough, was not universal. Whether the subject received any consideration from the authorities in England is a question on which only indirect evidence, so far as we have been able to discover, can be obtained.

In 1809 the forms observed in the ceremonial of electing a Speaker underwent important modifications. The vigour and fulness of the language between 1792 and the last mentioned year disappear, and as the change apparently took place in both provinces at

the same time, and resulted in the adoption by
both legislatures of a uniform style, it is fair to assume
that it was done in obedience to indentical orders, and
that those orders were made by competent authority.
But whatever may have been the opinion entertained in the mother country, there were men in the
colonies who not only had their doubts, but who found
an occasion to express them. Foremost among those
who did so was one who, having the courage of his convictions, boldly and in a very emphatic way took occasion
to declare his incredulity and to provoke a test. That
one was the Honourable William Warren Baldwin, better known in Upper Canada as Dr. Baldwin and as the
father of the late Honourable Robert Baldwin, both of
Toronto. The contrast is curious, for the former sought
to minimize the powers of the provincial legislature by
denying that it was a Parliament, while the latter in later
times succeeded in magnifying the provincial legislature
by grafting on it powers that were pre-eminently parliamentary. The interval that separated the two transactions
was one of thirty years, and may easily have passed out
of the recollection of all who had no particular reason for
retaining it in their memories. Nevertheless the doubt
of the father, though it eluded the mind of the son, may
have become blended with the traditions of the Colonial
office, and have found a handy place among the things
to be remembered. Perhaps that doubt, and the circumstances which attended its expression, were not without

influence on the transactions that occurred thirty years later. If a check had successfully been given to the appropriation by the Legislatures of Imperial privileges in 1809, why should not a check have been as effectually given in 1842 to the appropriation of Royal prerogatives? This inquiry will be dealt with at greater length in another chapter, when some allusion will be made to Sir Francis Hincks' observations on those events on the occasion of his address to the Irish National Society at Montreal in October last.

In 1812, when Major General Sir Isaac Brock was the Lieutenant Governor, and Great Britain and the United States stood face to face on the threshold of war, the following curious entries appear in the Journals of the Legislative Council and Assembly of Upper Canada :

HOUSE OF ASSEMBLY.

Tuesday, 11th February, 1812.

Read a letter from Alexander McDonell, Esq., a member representing the County of Glengarry, to His Honour, the Speaker, and it is in the following words :

YORK, 8th Sept., 1811.

SIR.—I feel it a duty incumbent on me to state to you, for the information of the Commons House of Assembly, that William Warren Baldwin, Esquire, has grossly and flagrantly violated the privileges of that Honourable Body by issuing as Deputy Clerk of the Crown, endorsing and putting into the hands of the Sheriff of the Home District, as Attorney at Law, a writ for the purpose of arresting my person about the 15th day of July now last past. The Deputy Sheriff (Mr. Hamilton) told Mr. Baldwin, when the latter put the writ in his hands, that, as a member of the House of Assembly, I was privileged from arrest ; this Mr. Baldwin denied, and insisted on his complying implicitly with the tenor of the writ. Mr. Hamilton declined, and referred the circumstance to the decision of the Sheriff who, being more versed in the duties of his office than Mr. Baldwin appears to have been in *his,* declined executing the writ.

This violation of privilege is more unpardonable in Mr. Baldwin than it could possibly be in any other attorney, for as Master in Chancery, he is the organ of communication from the Legislative Council to the House of Assembly, and at this late period he has the assurance to deny to the latter branch of the Legislature a privilege which they have already contended for, and which has invariably been admitted. Immaterial to the House that the writ has not been executed by the Sheriff Mr. Baldwin put the finishing touch to that part of the transaction which has a reference to his office as Attorney, and the infraction of privilege is as deeply wounded by his endorsing the writ as if my person had been taken into custody. To the decision of the House I submit the case, not doubting but every individual member will coincide with me in opinion that Mr. Baldwin in his threefold capacity of Deputy Clerk of the Crown, Attorney, and Master in Chancery, has violated the privileges of the House of Assembly.

(Signed),   ALEX. McDONELL.

"On motion of Mr. Gough, seconded by Captain Fraser, it was ordered that Thomas Hamilton, Deputy Sheriff, do attend at the Bar to-morrow."

The above seems not to have been the only offence that Dr. Baldwin had committed, for on the same day the following entry occurs :

"Mr. Gough again moved, seconded by Mr. Rodgers, that William Warren Baldwin, Esq., barrister, has been guilty of a false, scandalous, audacious, contemptuous libel of this House by publicly charging this House, in the hearing of several members thereof, with injustice to his father Robert Baldwin, one of the Commissioners for amending and repairing the public highways and roads for the District of Newcastle."

On the question being put on this remarkable resolution the yeas and nays were called for, when it was resolved in the affirmative in a house of twenty members, of whom seventeen were in attendance, by a majority of fourteen. The nays being Messrs. Mallory, Willcocks and Elliott.

"Then Mr. Gough, seconded by Mr. Rogers, moved that William Warren Baldwin, Esq., barrister, has been guilty of a breach of the privileges of this House by suing out a *capias*, and putting the same into the hands of the Sheriff of the Home District to execute against the person of Alexander McDonell, Esq., a member of this House.

" Which resolution was carried in the affirmative.

" Wednesday, 12th February, 1812.

" The Sergeant-at-Arms informed the Speaker that Mr. Thomas Hamilton attended at the Bar of the House in obedience to the order of yesterday.

" Mr. Thomas Hamilton was then called to the Bar of this House and, being examined by the House, declared that a writ of *capias ad respondendum* had been put into his hands by William Warren Baldwin, Esq., as Attorney against Alexander McDonell, Esq., a member of this House, on the 26th day of July 1811.

" That he did not execute this said writ, because he conceived Mr. McDonell to be privileged from arrest. That Mr. Baldwin urged him to make the said arrest, insisting that this House was not entitled to privilege, as being a House of Assembly and not a House of Parliament. The writ of *capias ad respondendum* was then produced by Mr. Hamilton, which was read at the Table and returned to him.

" Then Mr. Gough moved, seconded by Mr. Willcocks, that John Small, Esq., Clerk of the Crown, be ordered to attend at the Bar of this House at ten o'clock to-morrow morning. The same was ordered accordingly."

In passing it may be noted that Mr. Small, like Dr. Baldwin, is, we believe, remembered as a liberal politician, and, so far as a public official could be so, in sympathy with the reform party.

" Thursday, 13th February, 1812.

" The Sergeant-at-Arms informed the Speaker that John Small, Esq., attended at the Bar of this House in obedience to the order of yesterday.

" Being examined by the House, Mr. Small declared that the oath on which the *capias* against Alexander McDonell, a member of this House was issued, was taken by Mr. Jordan, and administered by himself ; that he had no intention to infringe upon any of the privileges of this House, and that if he had done so inadvertently he prayed that this House would pardon him.

Mr. Small's conditional " if " was somewhat roughly treated, for

" Mr. Gough, seconded by Mr. Rogers, moved that John Small, Esq., Clerk of the Crown, has been guilty of a breach of the privileges of this House by issuing from his office a *capias* against the person of Alexander McDonell, Esq., a member of this House, but Mr. Small having made an apology to the satisfaction of this House he be dismissed.

" The House accordingly resolved the same, and

" The Speaker informed Mr. Small of the said Resolution, and that, in consequence of his apology, he was permitted to retire from the Bar." But the proceedings in this curious matter were not yet at an end, for no sooner had Mr. Small retired than

"Mr. Gough again moved, seconded by Mr. Rogers, that a message be sent to the Legislative Council, with the Resolution of this House of the day before yesterday respecting the conduct of William Warren Baldwin, Esq., whom this House knows to be an officer attending their Honourable House as a Master in Chancery, assuring them of the reliance of this House that their Honourable House will proceed towards the delinquents as to their wisdom may seem meet and to justice may appertain."

"Which was ordered accordingly."

Turning to the journals of the Legislative Council we find that the Upper House was singularly in accord with the Lower one in regarding Mr. Baldwin's offence as very heinous indeed, and meriting all the punishment it was in the power of the Legislative Council to bestow.

"Journals of the Legislative Council

Thursday, 13th February, 1812.

PRESENT :

The Honourable MR. SCOTT, Speaker.

Honourable JAS. BABY.	Honorable JOHN McGILL.
ÆNEAS SHAW.	WM. CLAUS.

A deputation from the House of Assembly was announced.

It was admitted, and delivered at the Bar the following message:

' Mr. SPEAKER,—We are deputed by the House of Assembly to carry up to this Honourable House several resolutions which have passed the House respecting an officer of this House.'

Commons House of Assembly.

February 13, 1812.

SAMUEL STREET, Speaker."

The three resolutions are those of the House of Assembly of the 11th and 13th February, and are printed above.

"The resolutions having been ordered to lie on the table, the Legislative Council adjourned."

On the following day, Friday, February 14, the list of Members present in addition to those of the previous day includes the name of the Honourable Richard Cartwright.

" The message and resolutions of the House of Assembly on the conduct of William Warren Baldwin, Esq., were considered in a Committee of the Whole House," of which the Honourable Mr. Cartwright was the Chairman.

The following resolution was agreed to and sent to the Legislative Assembly:

" Legislative Council,

" February 14, 1812.

" Whereas certain resolutions of the Commons House

of Assembly, passed on the 11th day of February instant, signifying that William Warren Baldwin, Esquire, had incurred the displeasure of that House, were on the 13th instant communicated to this House by a message from the Commons House of Assembly at the Bar of this House,

" The Legislative Council, in consideration of the same, do

" Resolve, that the said William Warren Baldwin, Esq., be dismissed from the attendance on this House, and be no longer considered as an officer thereof, and that the Speaker do forthwith communicate this resolution to the Speaker of the Commons House of Assembly.

Attest.

(Signed),   JOHN POWELL, Clk. L. C."

It will be observed that the Legislative Council expressed no opinion on the question of privilege violated, or of disrespect shown. They made their resolve without descending to particulars or hampering themselves with reasons. Dr. Baldwin was evidently no favourite, and in those days of "stump law" it probably occasioned little surprise when the Council resolved to turn him out. The Doctor, besides being outside the official pale, was also one who indulged in a little independent thinking, and who probably could, if he so wished, be exceedingly disagreeable, if not absolutely contumacious. The Council apparently neither asked questions nor made inquiries. Action rather than investigation was their forte, and so at the bidding of the House of Assembly they degraded themselves by dismissing their officer. The act was one of suspicious severity, and seems to have been carried out without any reference to the question out of which it arose. Indeed, when it is borne in mind that the Chief Justice of the province was the Speaker of the Legislative Council, it almost justifies the impression that the Upper Canada legislature was most anxious to repress inquiry, and to intimidate, and run to earth any one who should venture to make it. Though the Legislative Council abstained from expressing an opinion, it evidently concurred with the House of Assembly in treating the question of the "privileges, immunities and powers" of their respective bodies as a sealed question, which no one should be permitted to open, and as a settled question, which even the courts of law should not be allowed to disturb by their intervention or destroy by their judgment.

Dr. Baldwin had not the privilege of a trial, for apparently he was not summoned by either house. There may have been reasons in policy for not questioning him directly, as he was known to hold inconvenient views on some matters of administration, and one, by way of specimen, he had communicated to Mr. Hamilton. The latter was evidently regarded as too destructive for discussion, and as it struck at the root of privilege it was dismissed by both houses. Nevertheless the question

F

was destined to re-assert itself thirty years afterwards, and at the end of twenty-four more years to become crystallized and preserved in an Imperial Statute whose short title is " The British North America Act," 1867.

There is a sequel to the proceedings above narrated which, though foreign to our subject, is interesting in relation to Dr. Baldwin, as it directly informs us for which of the two offences he was so summarily dismissed.   In the absence of the light thrown by this message on the transaction we might have doubted whether he was punished for acting courageously, or for speaking unadvisedly, as he was the object of a double attack.   At best it was a sorry proceeding in regard to which both Houses must have felt and ought to have looked dreadfully ashamed.

" Legislative Council Journals,

Saturday, February 15, 1812.

Members Present :—

The Honourable Thos. Scott, Speaker.

Honourable Messieurs

James Baby,   John McGill,

Richard Cartwright, William Claus.

Prayers were read.

A deputation from the House of Assembly was received with the following message :

" Mr. Speaker,—We are directed by the House of Assembly to inform the Honourable the Legislative Council,

" That the House of Assembly express the thanks of their House for the message of the Honourable the Legislative Council of yesterday so satisfactorily supporting the privileges of the Commons of Upper Canada, and to assure the Honourable the Legislative Council that the House of Assembly, though jealous of their privileges, disclaims whatever might appear vindictive, and that the House of Assembly feel a confidence that your Honourable House, from the prompt decision they made in support of those privileges, will be pleased to extend their mercy and accede to the earnest and unanimous solicitation of the Assembly that your Honourable House will be pleased to restore William Warren Baldwin, Esq., to his former situation in your Honourable House.

" Commons House of Assembly,

15th February, 1812.

SAMUEL STREET, Speaker."

Whereupon the following resolution was adopted and sent by message to the House of Assembly : " Resolved, that William Warren Baldwin, Esq., be restored accordingly to his former situation as an officer of this House."

Thus ends a curious episode in the Parliamentary history of the early days of Upper Canada. Before pursuing the subject it may be worthy of note that Dr. Baldwin either was not required, or, being required, would not apologize for what he had said and done. That abject ordeal was left to be undergone by less sturdy offenders. The chief delinquent was tolerably well known, and men generally understood what he could and what he could not be got to do. He was not the man to sacrifice his convictions, whether erroneous or the reverse, by apologizing for them ; hence he was, we suppose, studiously kept out of sight and out of hearing, beyond the reach alike of justice or of fair play.

By a pre-eminently tory legislature he was charged, condemned, punished and restored without a trial, or an apology for one. Doubtless policy was on their side who persecuted him. Apparently there was no law, and the lips of the judges gave no knowledge. Rough and ready legislation was one of the marks of the "good old times," and the "turn him out" expedient was by no means an unfamiliar one. It was a handy way of dealing with a difficulty, and represented what "Jimmy Wilson," a member of the old Upper Canada Legislature, used to describe as "stump law," being, as we conjecture, a primitive compound of arrogance and force.

CHAPTER IV.

ALTHOUGH the Legislative Assemblies of the two Provinces of Upper and Lower Canada subsequently adopted the like formulas when they presented their Speakers to the Governors for approval, they did not use the same prayer when they claimed the customary privileges, nor were their claims allowed in the same words; for the language used at the Western capital was more pointed and emphatic than the language employed at the Eastern one.

In 1801, the Honourable J. W. Smith, who for the second time had been elected Speaker of the House of Assembly of Upper Canada, claimed " in the name of the Assembly the freedom of speech, and generally all the like privileges and liberties as are enjoyed by the Commons of Great Britain our mother country."

In answer, the Speaker of the Legislative Council on behalf of the Lieutenant Governor said that the Assembly " may depend on the uninterrupted enjoyment of all its privileges," which was a very different kind of dependence from that promised at the opening of the first session of the Upper Canada legislature. In Lower Canada, Mr. Jean Antoine Panet was successively elected six times to be Speaker of the House of Assem-

bly.   On the first four occasions he uniformly petitioned
" for the privileges in use and which are of right claimed
by the Commons of Great Britain."   The answer he
received at the opening session in 1792 has already
been given.   On the second and two subsequent occasions he was uniformly answered by the Speaker of the
Legislative Council on behalf of the Governor in Chief
in the same words, viz.:   " That His Excellency in Her
Majesty's name allows them all their privileges in as full
and ample a manner as ever they have heretofore been
granted."   The value of the grant as expressed by command of Lieutenant Governor Sir Alured Clarke, has
already been dwelt on, nor do we see that its original
worth was increased by amplifying the words in which
it was subsequently repeated.   In both instances, however, an indirect rebuke was administered to the enthu-
siastic Governor Simcoe for his effort to bestow what he
had no authority to convey ; and also for describing by
implication the new constitution of Upper Canada as
" the image and transcript" of that of the mother
country, when in fact the points of dissimilarity were
quite as numerous as, and more important than, those of
resemblance.

The forms of petition above referred to appear to have
been continued in both Provinces till 1809, when a very
important and suggestive change took place.   Why the
alteration was introduced we have no means of knowing,
but it may fairly be assumed that a qualification so seri-

ous, even of a disputed advantage, was not made at the
instance of the Assemblies who would suffer loss by the
change. The alteration seemed to enter authoritatively
into our history, as if it had a right to be there, and, judging from the qualifications that followed, we are forced
to conclude that it was made in obedience to a remonstrance, in the nature of an order, from headquarters.
It is possible, however, that the colonists generally, were
indifferent alike to remonstrance or order, as they were
wholly disinclined to accept the conclusions to which
they led. Governor Simcoe had taught them to believe
that their legislatures, like the Parliament of England,
enjoyed the advantages which the latter possessed under
the common law, and that, irrespective of the ordeal of
petition, they really had, in virtue of ancient custom, and
without praying for them, the privileges in use, and
which are of right claimed by the Commons of the
United Kingdom. Being thus impressed, the members
of the Assemblies would have felt, and probably did feel,
much chagrined at the discovery that contrary opinions
were held elsewhere. That such contrary opinions were
so held was obviously the case, and that instructions in
harmony with them were issued seems almost, if not, absolutely certain. At all events impartial critics must arrive
at the conclusion that whether any rights analogous to
those enjoyed by the Parliament of the United Kingdom
could be claimed or not, it is clear that their quantity
was uncertain and their value doubtful.

The change appears to have first been made in 1809, when the Honourable Mr. Panet, for the fifth time, was elected to the office of Speaker of the House of Assembly of Lower Canada.   In his address to His Excellency on that occasion, Mr. Panet dropped the analogies he had previously employed, and made no allusions whatever to the Commons of Great Britain, or to the privileges in use and enjoyed by them. On the contrary he substituted for the vigour of the earlier prayer a modified formula of little value, but which we suppose must have been previously agreed on as a kind of lingual compromise between the old style and the new. Apparently the diluted prayer answered the purpose for which it was employed as it enabled the Speaker of the Legislative Council, by command of His Excellency to say something that meant nothing.   Whether satisfactory or the reverse, the new form was subsequently adopted by the Legislatures of Upper and Lower Canada, and it became the one in established use in both provinces when Speakers were chosen.   The change may, and probably at first did offend the ear, but the eye was conciliated, as no alteration was made in the pageant.   The drama of the " opening day " was preserved intact, and the Speaker's supplication for small mercies, like meandering music, had a beguiling effect, for it soothed the critics, and enforced silence.   No one cared to analyze the dialogue of the two Speakers, or curiously to inquire into the actual value of what was asked for and what was granted.

A settling day would come, but the time of its arrival was then far off, and there was no inclination to forestall the future. In the meanwhile the following took the place of the older form.

The Honourable Mr. Panet, " by humble petition on behalf of the Assembly, lays claim to all their rights and privileges, particularly that they may have liberty of speech for the better management of their debates, access to His Excellency's person on all seasonable occasions, and that their proceedings may receive from His Excellency the most favourable interpretation."

The petitions in both provinces were alike, but the answers which the Speakers, by direction of the Governors, returned to them were not the same.

In Lower Canada the answer ran thus : " The Governor in Chief will always respect the just rights and constitutional privileges of the Assembly," or the Governor in Chief " recognizes the accustomed and constitutional rights and privileges of the Assembly."

The words employed are different, neither have their meanings equal value, for to " respect" or to " recognize" are not equivalents for " granting " or " allowing." In Upper Canada the answers given by the Speakers of the Legislative Council by command were these : " The Lieutenant Governor "grants, and upon all occasions will recognize and allow, their constitutional privileges."

Unfortunately the Upper Canada journals of the pe-

riod, and for years afterwards were kept only in manuscript, and are incomplete. In some instances they cannot be found, as the originals were destroyed by fire,
and the copies were lost in transmission to England.
The journals of 1813, the war period, cannot be
accounted for. They are supposed to have fallen a prey
to the vigilance of some ship of war, or to have been
filched on their passage to England by an American pri-
vateer. We are enabled, however, from what remain to
arrive at a tolerably fair conclusion as to when the form
in Upper Canada was changed.

At the proceedings consequent on the election of a
Speaker in 1808 the early use was observed. The journals of both Houses for 1813, when a new Speaker
would have been elected, are missing; but the journals
of 1817, show that the change from the earlier to the
later form had previously been made, as the procedure
observed by the legislature of Upper Canada on that
occasion is in exact harmony with the procedure adopted
by the legislature of Lower Canada in 1809. Nevertheless, the House of Assembly of Upper Canada
evidently had not taken kindly to an abbreviation of their
privileges, and it is quite conceivable that they had a
particular dislike to the substitution of the new for the
old form, as the latter had a substantial value which the
former lacked. The whirligig of time, moreover, brought
to light unpleasant recollections, and disturbed a question
that many supposed had quietly been laid at rest. The

shield had been completely reversed, and Dr. Baldwin's
discomfiture in 1812 was followed by the Assembly's
humiliation in 1817. As a matter of curiosity, it would
be satisfactory to know how the result was brought
about ; and at whose instance and through whose intervention the Assemblymen were taught to know their
place. Was Dr. Baldwin himself the audacious leveller,
and did he fire the shot that damaged their pride, and
destroyed their privileges? Perhaps so ; for he was a
man of education and ability, and by no means disinclined to humble the exalted, or to give them, especially
if they were tories, severe lessons in humility. Moreover he was a liberal, and belonged to the reform party,
a party which at that time, and afterwards, was a good
deal discredited by the conduct of its allies. and thoroughly distrusted by its church and state opponents.
Authority, in such a crisis as dawned upon Canada in
the early part of 1812, would naturally, and perhaps
necessarily, become imperious, and, if such should have
been the case, all the estates of the legislature would
have caught the tone of the chief ruler. The reform
party, as then constituted, had reason to fear that the
Council and Assembly would exaggerate their powers
to the utmost, and glide with facility into practices that
might prove intolerant and would be oppressive. They
knew with what glibness such words as "sedition" and
"reform" were interchanged, and passed about ; nor
were they unaware of the fact that under the cover of

" loyalty " many wrongs had been wrought and many
inoffensive people threatened.

Taking counsel of their experience as well as of their
fears, liberals were to be excused in their efforts to restrain an influence which they had felt was arbitrary,
and believed was unjust. Hence they did what they
could to limit the privileges, and abase the powers, of a
body of representatives who were apt to show but scant
consideration to opinions not in accord with their own.
The episode, moreover, to which we are about to refer,
was fairly co-incident in time with the change of procedure.   In 1809 the new use was first observed at Quebec, and it is quite probable that the reason of the change
was also known at Toronto before 1811, when Dr. Baldwin issued his writ against Mr. McDonell ; an act which
in the following year, 1812, resulted in the proceedings
already related. All speculation, however, is idle ; though
why it should be so is a question that might possibly be
answered by another—why not recover what seems to
be, but is not, lost ?   The despatches, the directions, the
official and semi-official correspondence of that period, as
well as of earlier and later times, are much to be desired,
for they would supply a key to many of the doubtful,
and some of the obscure passages of our history.

Mr. Nichol in his day was evidently a prominent
member of the House of Assembly of Upper Canada, and,
like Mr. Gough in 1812, was apparently of the opinion
that the strongest words should be used everywhere, for

all purposes, and on every occasion. As will be seen presently, Mr. Nichol took refuge in an abstract resolution, hoping, as we gather by a highly emphasized declaration of opinion on the part of one branch of the Legislature, to recover and keep the privileges which no longer could legally be enjoyed by either branch.

"4th February, 1817.

"On motion of Mr. Nichol, seconded by Mr. Robinson:

"Allan McLean, Esq., knight, representing the County of Frontenac, was unanimously chosen Speaker.

"Then Mr. Nichol, seconded by Mr. Burwell, moved:

"That the Speaker do demand from the Lieutenant Governor the rights and privileges of this House as amply as they are enjoyed by the House of Commons of Great Britain"—*which was carried unanimously.*"

But His Excellency, though not intimidated, returned an evasive, rather than a spirited, answer to the "demand."

By command of His Excellency, the Speaker of the Legislative Council politely assured the Assembly "that their privileges should be respected." What those privileges were was a piece of information that all, no doubt, wished to get, but which none obtained. His Excellency probably took refuge in mystery, for his answer is a fair illustration of a strong meaning ambushed in soft words. Had the privileges been as "ample as those enjoyed by the House of Commons of Great Britain " His Excellency's answer would have been explicit instead of being, as it was, inconclusive, if not empty.   Such resolutions as Mr. Nichol's, and such unanimity as the Assembly showed in dealing with them, bore no fruit ; for thereafter and until 1841, the form introduced at Quebec in 1809 was also used at Toronto, and the older and more stimulating one was laid aside.   But, though the words were modified, the advantages they were intended to determine and bring to a close, were neither forgotten nor given up, for the privilege from arrest, together with the immunities and powers of Parliament, as originally claimed, were enjoyed and exercised as fully and effectually as if the right to do so were inherent, and had neither been denied nor questioned.   Time moved on ; Dr. Baldwin's challenge was forgotten, and the curious incident that attended and followed it had passed clean out of mind, but the cause of challenge remained, and waited only the occasion for a revival of the old contention.   Well nigh thirty years had elapsed from 1812 to the passing of the Act for re-uniting Upper and Lower Canada.   Among the particulars wherein the last-mentioned Act differed from the Act of the 31st Geo. 3rd, 1791, may be noted the fact that provision was made for the election of a Speaker, and also for the manner in which vacancies in the office of Speaker were to be filled.   The duty was to be discharged not as theretofore by direction of the Governor, but in virtue of the authority given by the

Imperial Act of 1840, 3rd and 4th Vict., cap. 35, and which is described in these words : " Be it enacted that the members of the Legislative Assembly of the Province of Canada shall, upon the first assembling after every general election, proceed forthwith to elect one of their number to be their Speaker." The authority thus given was to be exercised in accordance with a modern law, and not in deference to ancient custom. It was to be the first legislative act under the new constitutional charter, and it was to be done by the Assembly alone, without either vice-regal direction or vice-regal approval. Lord Sydenham was appointed Governor General for the express purpose of bringing about the re-union of the two Canadas, and of initiating an act that would not only include the terms and conditions of such union but would indicate the mode in which the two houses of the legislature should be constituted and continued. This was done with singular care and ability, and, as Lord Sydenham is supposed to have been the real author of that act, though his views were put into words by another hand, he must also be supposed to have known what he meant to do and on what lines he intended to carry on his work. Those who came into official contact with Lord Sydenham, albeit they are now few in number, will recall without difficulty the imperious character of his will and the strong vein of self-assertion that ran through his nature. When he had determined on a particular course, and when the time arrived for making such determination known, he would in the most direct way, in a few well chosen words, express his views and make some effort to enforce their meaning.   Hence we may be sure that he knew what he intended when he drew up his breviate of the Union Act, and also in what way he meant to carry out such intentions.

It should be borne in mind that, from Governor Simcoe to Lord Sydenham, no Governor had been sent to Upper Canada who had previously been a member of the House of Commons or who had been acquainted, either with ministerial tactics or Parliamentary procedure: The early Governors were generally soldiers of the revolutionary period who had fought against democracy in America and in Europe, while the later ones, having done service in the field and won national distinctions, were afterwards clothed with civil authority, which they generally discharged in a soldierly way.   Nor did the Governors-in-chief at Quebec differ very much from the Lieutenant Governors at Toronto, for although some of them were peers of high rank with seats in the House of Lords, and one of them, the Earl of Durham, had been a Cabinet Minister, they were, with few exceptions, Generals, and Generals rather than statesmen, whose education and experience savoured more of the barrack and of the camp; than of the House of Commons and the Cabinet.   We have seen how Governor Simcoe, who had sat in the House of Commons, commenced his rule, and in what light he regarded the legislature of Upper Canada. We have also seen that the analogies which he, with chivalrous devotion, sought to establish between the constitutions of Great Britain and Upper Canada were for the most part the creations of his imagination which could not be really established for lack of legal authority. In less than twenty years the powers and privileges which he thought he had the right to bestow with a free and open hand were reduced and diluted to a condition that rendered them harmless either for good or for evil. But the blow to local self-complacency which fell thirty-two years later was more effective than the one which struck the legislatures in 1809. On the latter occasion we learn particularly, by the teaching of a master highly skilled in the science of Parliamentary government, the exact as well as the relative measure of our legislative status. We learn, even when we close our eyes to the truth, that the three estates of the Canadian Legislature, though governing a territorial area that was formerly ruled by two separate legislatures, were still limited in matters of administration by geographical boundaries. They could not overstep the municipal lines by which they were enclosed. The re-united Provinces may have seemed more imposing, and may have received more consideration than the separated ones, nevertheless, beyond the Canadian boundary, the larger Legislature had no more power than the smaller ones. It was not in the statutory sense a " Parliament,"

but something subordinate to it, which, by way of distinction, had been styled in the English law a " Legislature."
Its proportions, no doubt, had been enlarged, but they
rested on the old foundations—hence its increased size,
though it added to its importance, did not change its
species. Like its predecessors, it continued to be exactly
what the Parliament of the United Kingdom had declared
it to be, a " Legislature " and a legislature only.

In writing of the early limits by which the power and
authority of what may be termed the experimental provinces of British North America was restrained and cir-
cumscribed, it would be instructive, and it ought to be possible, to learn by whom and under what authority those
old lines in their more minute bearings were suggested,
and by whose hand they were traced. The inquiry
belongs to the early history of the British possessions
in North America on which stray books and forgotten
newspapers shed but feeble light. They do not particu-
larize the source, neither do they afford any clue to the
authors of many matters on which it would be desirable
to possess information. One would like, so to speak, to
have a pass to the green-room of the play, to be introduced to the author, to chat with the prompter, and to
look at the pageant from the side scenes, as well as in
front of the stage. It would be interesting to see the
manager, to listen to his directions, to note the actors,
and even to glimpse " the properties." The early Canadian drama, homely as it may have been, suggests

many subjects of inquiry. A search among letters and papers might disclose information that would be curious, and perhaps valuable. In any case it ought to be within reach. It would be interesting, for example, to learn how it came about that Governor Simcoe took for his style a royal pattern, and appropriated the language of his Sovereign, together with the prerogatives of the Crown, when he officially met for the first time the Legislative Council and Assembly of Upper Canada. The constitutional act could not have been his directory, for no hint, of such a ceremonial as he and his successors adopted is to be found in any of its provisions. He may, of course, have been authoritatively instructed as to the forms he should use, and perhaps plainly told in what way, and to what extent, he was to imitate the manner and use the language of his Royal Master. But if such were the case, those instructions should be accessible, if not in this country, at least among the records of the Colonial department, or in some office connected with the Royal household. It is, however, difficult to believe that the ceremonial which Governor Simcoe observed was ordered by the King, or suggested by His ministers, for so far as we have been able to discover, neither the Sovereign nor the statesmen of England had ever given any directions on the subject. Both, no doubt, must have acquiesced in what was done, though there is reason for believing that neither assented to what was said. They uniformly distinguished between " Parlia-

ment" and "Legislature," and quietly withheld from the
latter those rights and privileges which time, struggle and
use have inseparably associated with the former.   No
doubt Governor Simcoe had to find some way of com-
municating with the two Houses of the Legislature, and
we venture to think he could as legally have done so
by message as by speech, by his Secretary as in person.
He chose the latter course for what, no doubt, he thought
constitutional reasons.   He had to establish a precedent,
and the form he thought fit to adopt was convenient and
imposing, while it veiled some serious fallacies, which
eventually became the subjects of controversy in Canada,
and possibly also of correspondence with the home
government.

In the meanwhile the Legislature, for no particular
reason that we can discover, fell into the habit of declar-
ing itself to be a Parliament, and consequently, in imitation of the English use, it followed that it could not perfect the resemblance, or begin its work, without the
assembling in one chamber of the three estates of the
legislature.   The English original was carefully studied,
and the lessons in the laws of analogy and imitation were
learned with amusing exactness.   This gathering in one
chamber of the Governor, of the "great men" and the
"Knights, Citizens and Burgesses" included ceremonies
which could not be carried out in a picturesque way
without the aid of ushers and sergeants, and so it was
that the Upper house received the garnish of a black

rod, and the Lower one the glitter of a gilt mace, while the sanctity of religion was gracefully recognized in the appointments of a chaplain to each. With such picturesque representatives of dignity, learning and religion, the two houses in their scenic surroundings were brought into a state of weak resemblance with the houses of Lords and Commons. Men made no deep scrutiny into the meaning of terms which they did not seem called upon to examine, or to refer to statutes and dictionaries that they might contrast, as well as compare, the meaning of words. Having a real legislature composed of three parts they easily gave it an interchangeable name, with brevet rank, and crowned both by adding outward symbols of striking significance. Then it should also be borne in mind that the phraseology of the legislature, and of proclamations relating to it, was in like manner brought into harmony with the language used on like subjects and occasions in the Mother Country. The former may be read in the courtly dialogues that took place in the Legislative Council at the opening of a new " Parliament," or at the closing of a session ; and the latter will be seen in those stereotyped proclamations, issued at special intervals, wherein the Lieutenant Governor summoned his " well beloved and faithful the Legislative Councillors of the Province of Upper Canada, and the Knights, Citizens and Burgesses elected to serve in the Legislative Assembly of our said Province, summoned and called to a meeting of the Provincial Parliament of our said

Province," and in these and other ways the idea was formulated and became a conviction that the legislature was a " Parliament." Thus the fallacy was encouraged and hardened by such ceremonials, and it was pre-served and carried out in proclamations and probably in less authoritative public documents. It was crystal-lized in colloquies and repeated in printed papers, and hence it followed that the ordinary talk of the com-mon people gave force and consistency to all that had been said and done. The consequences were natural enough ; for the habit of thought thus acquired was transmitted from generation to generation with contin-ually increasing distinctness. The words " Parliament " and " Legislature " came to be regarded as synonymous expressions, but the former, being the more imposing of the two, was used with pretentious ostentation, while the latter fell into comparative obscurity and well nigh dropped out of the Canadian vocabulary.

But this view of the question, which from a careless habit had almost acquired the force of law, received a rude shock on the arrival of Lord Sydenham, when the first session of the Legislature of reunited Canada assem-bled at Kingston.

A few preliminary words of explanation are necessary for the information of such persons as are unacquainted with the facts of the case, or from whose memory they have escaped.

The constitutional act of 1791 contained no directions as to the way in which a Speaker of the House of Assembly was to be elected. Wherefore Governor Simcoe naturally enough fell back on the forms observed in such cases by the House of Commons. Contact with these forms suggested that the rule of analogy should be carried thoroughly out. These included the presentation of the person chosen to His Excellency for approval, as well as for the bestowal of privileges, including the particular one that was subsequently challenged, viz. : freedom from arrest.

We have noted elsewhere that the last mentioned privilege having been improperly allowed, was cleverly and incidentally, though not specifically and in exact words, withdrawn. A weaker form of expression was substituted for the one first employed, in which no trace could be found of any reference to the privileges that Dr. Baldwin had challenged, and had resisted unsuccessfully. In fact it was generalized into space, and lost in the effort to interpret it anew. But if the members of the legislature surrendered a privilege it was not intended they should possess, the Crown also was about to lose a function which it neither asked for, nor wanted, but which it acquired, it would seem, in virtue of one of those acts of imitation which Governor Simcoe had introduced and which his successors had continued. The change arose in this way :

On the 2nd November, 1827, the Honourable Louis Joseph Papineau, who had continuously been Speaker of the House of Assembly of Lower Canada from 1815, was re-elected to that honourable office.   It so happened that differences of a bitter personal character had arisen between him and the Earl of Dalhousie, the then Governor in Chief.   The latter no doubt was exceed· ingly angry, perhaps he had cause to be so, but he took a passionate way of showing his resentment.   When Mr. Papineau on the following day, in accordance with custom, presented himself at the bar of the Legislative Council for His Excellency's approval ; the Speaker of the Legislative Council, by command of the Governor, said, " That the choice made by the Assembly was dis- allowed, and they were to go back and choose another person for their Speaker." This slap in the face, of which only two examples were found in English history, one in the Tudor and the other in the Stuart times, could only be answered by the Assembly in one way, and that way was adopted by their immediately re-electing Mr. Papineau.   Lord Dalhousie was thus ignominiously thrust to the wall.   Only one course was open to him, and that he took.   He prorogued the Legislature at once by proclamation, resigned his office, and went home. He was succeeded by the Lieutenant Governor of Nova Scotia, Sir James Kempt, who had no objection to offer to Mr. Papineau's election as Speaker.   As an incident of the affair, and consequent on it, certain declaratory resolutions were adopted by the Assembly which were true enough in relation to a Legislature created by a special statute, but which would not have escaped criticism had that Legislature been a Parliament. Their adoption destroyed a fiction that apparently had been firmly believed and fondly cherished, viz. : that the Legislature of Lower Canada, like the Imperial Parliament, derived its privileges from the common law of England, whereas the resolutions, by implication if not actually, declared that it was created by a special statute, and that therefore it was controlled by the obligations of a modern law and not by forms derived only from ancient custom.

Lord Dalhousie's petulant act, followed as it was by resolutions of doubtful wisdom, led, it is believed, to the alteration in the procedure that took place in subsequent times. The late Mr. Cuvillier, who had charge of the matter in the Lower Canada House of Assembly, declared in one of his resolutions, all of which were adopted by that House, that " the approval of Mr. Speaker by His Excellency was an act of courtesy and not an obligation of law." This no doubt was true, for as the legislature of Lower Canada was not an outgrowth of the common law of England, but a creation of the Act 31st George the Third, it followed that it was not immemorial use, but exact law, that was to control the proceedings. As the obligation of law could not be found in the constitutional act, neither could any practice be insisted on that was not traceable to and authorized by that act. Presenting the Speaker for approval, so the allegation ran, was merely a matter of local spontaneity, and expressed only a compliment and not an obligation. The act of grace having been abused by the Governor, it was alleged could be withdrawn by the Assembly, and as we shall see presently it was withdrawn not only by the Assembly, so far as a declaratory resolution could effect that end, but by the Imperial Parliament in deference to the desire expressed in that resolution. The supreme authority thus concurred with the Lower Canada Assembly in opinion that the latter was governed by law and not by custom and usage. Whether the Assembly acted wisely is a question that scarcely admits of doubt, for if there was anything to lose the loss was theirs. They could no longer pose, as they had done, on the common law, and on the constitutional act. Having a choice to make, they deliberately cut the painter, if such existed, that fastened them to the former, and in the irritation of the moment, and for a mere passing triumph, gave up all claims, whether well founded or the reverse, to the use and custom of the ages. Thus in appealing to the clear and written law they surrendered their right, if they had any, as theretofore they thought they had, to walk in the " deep-trod footmarks of ancient custom." No such occasion was likely again to arise, for the stock of petulant rulers is limited ; and as the victory lay with the Assembly it would have been wiser not to have wasted their strength by passing declaratory resolutions, whose effect was to lower their own status, and to weaken, if not to destroy, the line of argument that could be urged as a basis whereon to rest their claim to privileges. The use to which their resolves was put was seen in the Act for reuniting the Canadas, for it gave colour and authority to the attitude taken by Lord Sydenham when the first Speaker of the Legislative Assembly of the United Provinces was chosen.

The thirty-third Section of the Act reuniting the two Canadas runs thus: "33. And be it enacted, that the members of the Legislative Assembly of the Province of Canada shall upon the first assembly after any general election proceed forthwith to elect one of their number to be Speaker, and in case of his death, resignation or removal by a vote of the said Legislative Assembly, the said members shall forthwith proceed to elect another of such members to be Speaker, and the Speaker so elected shall preside at all meetings of the said Legislative Assembly."

The House of Assembly met on the 14th June, 1841, when the proceedings which theretofore had been observed in Upper and Lower Canada were seriously changed, and changed, be it noted, in obedience to the terms of the act from which the last mentioned clause is taken. The Journals read thus: "After the members were sworn by the commissioners appointed for that purpose, the proclamation summoning the legislature for the despatch of business was read by the Clerk and

" The thirty-third Section of the Imperial Act 3rd and 4th Victoria, Cap. 35, having been also read,

" It was then moved by Mr. A. N. MORIN, seconded by Mr. WILLIAM HAMILTON MERRITT :

"That Mr. Austin Cuvillier be their speaker, which was unanimously agreed to.

" The Speaker was then conducted to his chair with the usual ceremonies."

" It was then moved by Mr. SIMPSON, seconded by MR. JOHN S. MACDONALD :

"That the House adjourn till to-morrow at two o'clock P.M.

" Upon which the House divided.

" For the yeas, Mr. Aylwin (Teller), 47.

" For the nays, Mr. Manahan (Teller), 27."

"So it was again resolved in the affirmative and the House adjourned."

The crop of debates that grew round the above proceedings are alike interesting and suggestive, for the changed procedure is distinctly traceable to the interpretation given by the Imperial Parliament to Mr. Cuvillier's resolution of 1827. Consequently the new act made a very important alteration, for which the Assembly was wholly unprepared, in the use which had theretofore been observed; nor was it a subject of wonder that such surprise should have found animated expression in debate. Perhaps such debates might not have arisen, or having arisen might have taken a new direction, had the antecedent question " Are Legisla-

tures Parliaments ? " been asked and answered. On this
point it is needless to inquire. The light of later legislation had not then shone on it, and consequently the
Assemblymen of that period would in all probability have been governed by local precedents, and
have declined to discuss hypercritical definitions. Lord
Sydenham, no doubt, had reason for the course he took.
At all events he had the law with him ; but whether he
wished to conciliate the Assembly by thus abrogating an
executive function, or whether by anticipation he saw
the Imperial distinctions that were to be drawn twenty-
six years later, we have no means of knowing. All that
need be said is, that in his speech on opening the session
His Excellency, in a very marked way, distinguished
between " Legislature " and " Parliament," and only
used the latter word when he referred to the Parliament
of the United Kingdom. A very discursive and a very
lengthy debate followed the motion for adjournment.
Mr. Aylwin, after referring to the thirty-third section
of the Union Act, objected that the Parliament had not
assembled, as His Excellency had not met the Assembly
together " with the great men of the land " obviously
meaning the Legislative Council. " If," said Mr.
Aylwin with playful force, " if we are as badly off as a
starved out jury, after two days confinement, we cannot
adjourn. If the law of Parliament has been altered,
Her Majesty's advisers should show wherein it has been
altered."

" Mr. Viger inquired, What is the commencement of a Parliament? It is to be opened by the attendance of the Sovereign, or of the Sovereign's representative, after the two Houses have been assembled by proclamation. Then the Sovereign commands the Commons to proceed to the election of their Speaker. If you introduce irregularities, what irregularities will you not pass over! I tremble for the consequences!"

" Mr. Morin said, We have not the power of abolishing the common law of England. By that law the King comes down to the House of Parliament and commands the Commons to proceed to the choice of a Speaker."

" Mr. Draper said that the 33rd section of the statute for the reunion of the Canadas had made it unnecessary that our choice of a Speaker should receive the sanction of Royalty." This remark may have recalled to Mr. Cuvillier's mind his contention in 1827, when he informed Lord Dalhousie that the presentation of the Speaker for approval was a matter of compliment and not an obligation of law. Mr. Hincks " believed that to-day's proceedings must be null and void. It is evident that His Excellency has been badly advised. The only way left is to adjourn Parliament until to-morrow, since Her Majesty's legal advisers decline to bring forward any precedent."

Mr. Boswell said " we have made a Speaker conformably to the Act, but, though the Speaker be chosen, Parliament has not met. I see no way unless His Excellency be advised to come down to us."

But that was precisely the sort of advice that Lord Sydenham would have declined to follow, for His Lordship could not easily be taken where he was unwilling to go. So, having elected their Speaker according to law, the Assembly adjourned to the next day, when His Excellency opened the Legislature by a gracious speech to both Houses, having, however, previously assured the House of Assembly, in answer to the stereotyped prayer preferred by their Speaker, that "he grants and on all occasions will recognize and allow their constitutional privileges."

It was then fifty years since the Act 31 George the Third was passed, and only one year less since Governor Simcoe, supposing that he had the right to do so, went through the form of conferring on the members of the Upper Canada legislature privileges, similar to those at that time enjoyed by the members of the Parliament of Great Britain. Eighteen years later, in 1809, these privileges were explained away, by substituting for the clear form of words in which they were at first conferred, a string of phrases whose value was determined by popular superstition rather than by local precedents or exact law.

Three years later, in 1812, Dr. Baldwin sought to bring the privilege question to an issue. He had the hardihood to promote the arrest of a member of the Assembly for debt, asserting as his reason for doing so that such persons were not privileged, as "an Assembly was not a Parliament." Fifteen years later, in 1827, the House of

Assembly of Lower Canada, on the resolution of Mr. Cuvillier, declared that the initiatory proceedings on choosing a Speaker were obligations of law, and not matters of compliment. In other words, that they were done under the authority of a special statute and not in virtue of ancient custom and usage; and, lastly, Lord Sydenham's having gathered together the broken threads of past controversies, and probably being also aware, from reference to sources of information within his, but out of our, reach, what were the intentions of the Parliament of Great Britain in 1791, and as well as what were the intentions of the Parliament of the United Kingdom in 1840, and also how one Act had been, and how the other would be, interpreted by the authorities in England, put a construction on the law that was not only agreeable to his own views, but to theirs also who had promoted and who had passed that law. His Excellency, probably without being aware of it, acted in accordance with the opinion expressed by Dr. Baldwin, thirty years earlier, " that an Assembly was not a Parliament," and with the opinion expressed by Mr. Cuvillier, fourteen years earlier, that proceedings " that were not obligations of law " could not be enforced as matters of custom. Such views apparently harmonized with, and seemed to control, Lord Sydenham's conduct. " If," (we may imagine His Excellency to have said), " the Legislature of Upper Canada was only the ' creation of a statute, and if the Legislature of Lower

" Canada was only the creation of a statute, then the
" Legislature of reunited Canada could claim no higher
" rank and rest on no other basis than the Act which
" authorized, and called it into existence.   Consequently
" the members of such Legislature collectively and indi-
" vidually may not claim, nor may I bestow, any privi-
" leges, any immunities, or any powers, that are not
" plainly found in the written constitution as it is dis-
" tinctly set forth in the law entitled ' *An Act to Reunite*
" *the Provinces of Upper and Lower Canada and for*
" *the Government of Canada,*' because they have no
" prescriptive, but only statutory rights."

Having noted what was done at the opening sessions
of the Legislatures of Upper and Lower Canada in 1792,
and also what was done by the Legislative Assembly of
re-united Canada in 1841, it remains only to direct attention to the proceedings at the first session of the Parliament of Canada in 1867, when the newly-elected Speaker
of the Commons, accompanied by the members of that
House, in obedience to the command of the Governor
General, attended at the bar of the Senate.

If a doubtful value attached to proceedings theretofore
had by successive Governors, it might have been expected that, when the irregularities had been cleared
away by statute, the course to be followed would have
been sufficiently plain.   And so it was, but it did not
take the direction which many persons imagined it ought
to have taken.   " The British North America Act 1867."

seems to have been drawn for the express purpose of
meeting difficulties and removing doubts. Certainly it
sets at rest all such contentions as Dr. Baldwin had
made. The legislature of Canada was succeeded by the
Parliament of Canada, and this succession included an
answer, emphatically given in the negative, by the Parliament of the United Kingdom to the important question
" are Legislatures Parliaments ? " The Queen, the Lords
and the Commons say no, they are not. The change
from a doubtful and obscure to an exact and statutory
status it was commonly supposed would make new
formulas necessary, or possibly revive some of those early
ones that had evidently been disallowed. Thus the new
departure included several points of speculative interest,
and in the minds of some persons gave a novel attrac-
tion to those occasions, and to those ceremonies, where
the gracious utterances of Her Majesty's representative
had theretofore been regarded as meaningless, and consequently valueless. Now, however, for the first time in
colonial history, " the privileges, immunities and powers "
exercised by the Commons House of Parliament of the
United Kingdom and by the Members thereof, were bestowed on the supreme legislature of Canada. What
these included we learn from the Lords' Journals of 1874.
The entry is as follows. When Mr. Brand was re elected
Speaker of the House of Commons, after the Lord Chancellor, in Her Majesty's behalf, had approved of the
choice, Mr. Brand said :

"I submit myself with all humility and gratitude to
Her Majesty's gracious commands, and it is now my
duty, in the name and on the behalf of the Commons of
the United Kingdom, to lay claim, by humble Petition to
Her Majesty, to all their ancient and undoubted rights
and privileges, particularly to freedom of speech in debate; to freedom from arrest of their persons and servants; to free access to Her Majesty when occasion shall
require; and that the most favourable construction should
be put upon all their proceedings, and with regard to
myself I pray that if any error should be committed it
may be imputed to myself, and not to Her Majesty's
loyal Commons."

By Her Majesty's command the Lord Chancellor
"most readily confirmed all the rights and privileges
which had ever been granted."

Such, as Mr. Brand enumerated, were the privileges
acquired by the Parliament of Canada under "The
British North America Act, 1867." No change, however,
was made in the ceremonial of electing the Speaker,
for the mode prescribed in the Imperial Statute of 1840,
though amplified in practice, was continued in that of
1867. There was no difference in the words of the address of the member elected to be the Speaker, and there
was no enlargement of his usual prayer, when on behalf
of the Commons, he made his petition for privileges. The
qualified, and almost meaningless, form that was introduced in 1809 and repeated till 1863 was continued

without alteration in 1867. The opening ceremony would of course have seemed incomplete without the usual accompaniments, and so the time-honoured dialogue between the Speakers of the two Houses was repeated in the old words. It was evident the authorities were of opinion that the enlarged powers conferred by "The British North America Act, 1867," did not render necessary a correspondingly enlarged mode of expressing them. Nevertheless, at first sight, the occasion, its analogies, and its increased authority, very naturally suggested as close an approach as possible to the forms and words observed at the like ceremonies by the Imperial Parliament. The doubt however disappears before a moment's reflection. The Parliament of Canada possessed the privileges they needed under a better title than the good will and condescension of the most exalted Viceroy, for they held them under the authority of a law passed by the Parliament of the United Kingdom. They were therefore not disquieted by the continuance of the modified formula, nor were they disappointed that the early style of 1792 was not revived in 1867.

With the passing of "The British North America Act, 1867," and the creation of the Parliament of Canada, the time came when all controversy should cease as to the exercise of the "privileges, immunities and powers" of Parliament. Thenceforward they were to be held by a title that could neither be challenged nor counterfeited. They were acquired by an Imperial Statute, and could neither be altered nor qualified by any authority lower than the one which had conferred them. Indeed the ceremonial observed by the Parliament of Canada is an idle, and, but for the pageant, which from the force of association few persons would be willing to miss, an unmeaning one. The Governor cannot take exception to the person chosen by the Commons to be their Speaker, neither will it avail him to refuse the Speaker's supplication for small privileges, since the Imperial Act grants these minor favours, and some others of a much higher and more important character. The question arises, if for the exercise of these " privileges, immunities and powers" by the Parliament of Canada a statute of the Parliament of the United Kingdom was necessary, how, in the absence of the like instrument, can the subordinate Legislatures in Canada take authority to exercise the like "privileges, immunities and powers?" The question is pertinent, and can, as we venture to think, receive only one answer.

CHAPTER V.

THE story of his failure to restrain the House of Assembly of Upper Canada from using privileges and exemptions that solely belonged to the Parliament of the United Kingdom no doubt remained indelibly impressed on Dr. Baldwin's memory. It was too personal and too spiteful to be forgotten by one who had sufffered in his effort to give effect to what he believed was lawful and right. But what Dr. Baldwin had good reason to remember, other people were easily excused for forgetting, for they lacked, at the early period of our history. those daily criticisms that now fidget their readers about times past, present and future. The inhabitants of the "Town of York" were much to be envied, for they escaped some of the miseries to which their successors at Toronto are exposed. In their simplicity they thought, as some think now, there were greater blessings in this world than a multiplicity of newspapers. One, in those days sufficed to furnish them with information, and they seem not to have required a second to suggest incredulity, or a third to supply invective. At that sylvan period there were no publishers, and apparently there was neither occasion nor desire for any. The public records were not printed then, nor till years later, and consequently such irritating and debatable documents as public accounts, and departmental papers, were snugly lodged with the spiders in peaceful pigeon holes, and, being well entrenched in dust, were not likely to be interfered with by man. Such privacy, however, was of the less consequence since they were rarely examined and never explained. The finance ministers of that period were ill skilled in figures, and there were no deputies to supply what was lacking in the chiefs. Moreover, the common folk of the earlier epoch possessed great faith, and were little given to pry. Incredulity is the development of later days, when men persist in making their neighbours uncomfortable by not taking everything for granted, and insisting that sight is a condition of faith. Such sceptics obstinately persevere in not regarding the public accounts, for example, as veiled mysteries, but rather as exhibits to be critically analyzed by experts, to be threshed, winnowed and scattered broadcast, like seed from a full hand, into the moral soil of the country, and there left to instruct and worry the electorate. In the good old times inquisitive-ness was not pointed with scepticism, for men were prone to believe whatever they saw in print. Doubt is a product of later days, and belongs to the progressive period of railways, photographs and telephones. Print had not become a local power sixty-seven years ago, and, consequently, Dr. Baldwin's grievance was not leaded in repeating type, or preserved in manifold papers.

Between the angry episode on Parliamentary privileges
in 1811 and the famous resolutions on Parliamentary
responsibility in 1841, there was time enough for many
events to happen, to be discussed, and to pass into
oblivion. Opinion, moreover, had wrought several
changes which found expression in an equal number of
surprises. The tories of the early period had disap-
peared, like the Dodo, or, if specimens were here and
there preserved, they resembled those species hat are
only found in petrifactions and fossils. The reformers,
on the other hand, exhibited, as is their habit, an
uncomfortable vitality. They were so thoroughly im-
pregnated with the principle of growth and animation as
to "wax fat and kick." Thus they not only spread
themselves out with a view to win, but eventually, to
the amazement of the tories, acquired control of the
situation. The heirs of the latter, like their English
namesakes, were obliged to hold their titles in suspense,
and ambush themselves behind the colourless designation
of conservative. Dr. Baldwin had been a reformer during
the dark era, when it was alike unfashionable and com-
promising to be so. He was a reformer when such a confession of political faith meant social exclusion and political outlawry. Taking into account the disabilities to
which his opinions exposed him, it was natural, and perhaps wise, on his part to do what in him lay, to pay the
grudge he owed to his political enemies, and to do it with
coin of any denomination. To this end he sought to

abridge the powers, and abate the pretentions of those
in authority, to arraign all analogies or conceits, whether
real or fictitious, before the proper tribunal, and, if found
to be shams, to strip the wearers in the open courts, and
admonish them in the set forms of law not to offend
again.   Dr. Baldwin failed to effect his ambitious purpose in the way he intended to do so.   The interests he
assailed were too strong for him, and so he was answered
with rough words.   His indictment was quashed, and a
question that ought calmly to have been settled by the
judges was rudely hustled out of court.   The assumption
of privileges having been as passionately affirmed as it
had been violently denied was comfortably enjoyed.
It would really seem that the Chief Justice was in league
with the Legislature in stifling inquiry and in asserting
his, and their, supremacy over the law.   Against such
odds there was little hope of renewing the combat with
success.   No one again adventured to do so.   Reform
virtue subsided into indifference, and the creditors of
impecunious members of the Legislature into dissatisfied
students of privilege.   The arbitrary rule that individuals
having seats in the Assemblies were above the law had
been substituted for the law, and objectors found it was
only lost labour to dwell on the incompetence of the
authority by which such substitution had been made.
A new and pleasant way had been discovered for paying,
or for postponing old debts, and the discoverers, in
spite of Dr. Baldwin's animated protest, were by no

means inclined to part with the patent that supplied them with such peculiar advantages.

One of the consequences that followed the rise into power of the reform party became apparent thirty years afterwards. Dr. Baldwin had either changed his early opinions or he held them in suspense. It may have been that to the Doctor's medical eye the diagnosis presented new features and required a course of treatment with which he was unacquainted when he first examined his patient. Be this as it may, there can be little doubt that the policy of success was susceptible of very different combinations to those required by the experience of failure. Elation and not depression characterized the new departure, for the popular aim was not only to retain privileges that had never been successfully challenged but to invade prerogatives which theretofore had been jealously guarded. It would, under such circumstances, have been highly inconvenient to revive an episode in colonial history, where a hereditary reformer of the purest type advocated a system of shrinkage in what were then regarded as constitutional rights, because he was now called upon to promote a system of expansion, by seizing prerogatives that were generally looked upon as royal possessions. The faculty of forgetfulness came then, as it often does now, as a blessing to men. No one, save Dr. Baldwin himself, in all probability, remembered the civil process of 1811, or the violent proceedings to which the service of it gave rise in 1812. The able and painstaking son seems, if not to have changed the opinions of the conscientious and defiant father, at least to have set a seal on his lips and lulled his patriotic conscience into a state of sympathetic repose. Thus were Dr. Baldwin, the unsuccessful advocate of Legislative contraction, and his son, Mr. Robert Baldwin, the successful champion of Legislative expansion, brought into accord. The pessimist of 1811 and the optimist of 1841 compared their contrary experiences and discovered that, by diverging paths, they had reached or might reach a common end. The contrast, moreover, might be carried further, for the father failed while the son succeeded. Moreover the father failed, though the law would probably have sustained him, while the son succeeded without the aid of law, in the very teeth of authority, and in spite of every form of official prejudice, by means of a declaratory resolution only. Nevertheless, though the subjects and proceedings were different, the reasons that determined them were nearly alike. Political rapacity and a greed for rule clings to the roots of both events. In 1811 the Assembly had shown a resolute unwillingness to surrender a privilege which they clearly had no right to possess but were determined to keep, while in 1841 they were as fully bent on appropriating powers which had never been bestowed, and which the Crown had shewn a marked indisposition to grant. "Fortune favours the bold." The representatives of the Canadian people shewed spirit alike in their defence and in their attack, and eventually appropriated the fruits of resolute tenacity and successful aggression.

Between the years 1811 and 1841 public opinion in Canada underwent several transformations. The Colonial legislatures, having outgrown their swaddling clothes, began to articulate their wishes plainly, and, after the manner of exuberant youth, aspired to a higher status and more consideration. In their tender childhood they had found themselves equal to the emergency of appropriating privileges that did not belong to them ; and now, in their dawning manhood, they resolved to acquire prerogatives that belonged to some one else. But, before the grand panacea for colonial ills was invented, before the resolutions on the subject of "responsible government" were adopted, some intermediate occurrences took place that deserve to be noted, for they throw much light on the history and progress of public opinion in Canada.

The immigration that followed the peace of 1815 brought into British North America new classes of settlers from the United States and from Europe. The former country contributed a good many people who were practically familiar with the working of republican institutions and generally preferred a democratic to a monarchical form of government. In like manner, the British Islands poured out thousands whom war and its exactions had made miserable, to seek in the new world the happiness and plenty that had eluded them in the old one. Such persons had been, for the most part, actively or passively at war with the age and with its institutions, so that, whatever hue their political opinions had acquired was deeply tinged with levelling, not to say revolutionary, pigments. Such persons belonged to the open-mouthed classes who said what they had to say in loud tones and few words, and those words, from force of habit, and perhaps a natural instinct, were usually directed against the government. Thus passionate forms of expression became common, for men who, in the old world, had learned to believe that kings were the root of all evil and the authors of all ills, were not likely in the new one to discipline their speech to those tones of heartiness which the loyalists habitually used when addressing their Sovereign through his accreditated representative. The new opinions changed the old manners, while they gave rise to fears that were too acute to be shadowy, as to what would come next. True to their hereditary instincts, the tories were equally ready to threaten or to fight, but they would not parley with men whose political objects were pursued, and whose political aims were reached, by ways that they thought were crooked and by means which they regarded as evil. Consequently, they stood aloof and looked with disdain, not unmingled with dread, on the educators of the passing and approaching era. In the meanwhile republican experiences and radical opinions became more intensely active. Their owners and authors joined hands, and by their union

made alarming headway in a Province that was euphe-
mistically called " the retreat of suffering loyalty."   But
the recollection of the cost at which " the retreat " had
been acquired worked like a charm.   The tories had no
wish to buy over again what had once been purchased
with great personal sacrifices.   They could no longer look
on passing events with stoical indifference.   On the
contrary, an occasion arose when they became boister-
ously indignant, and loudly claimed the interference of
the Legislature.   The cause of alarm was that the
objectionable immigrants from over the border and across
the sea, not only had the hardihood to complain of
grievances, but had the temerity to discuss them at
"A Convention of Delegates."   A convention of
Delegates !   The apparition was too horrible to be
endured.   It recalled to the minds of the loyalists one of
the many mischievous contrivances which it was hoped
they had left, with their estates, behind them, when they
abandoned republican for monarchial America.   Their
sacrifice would have been dearly purchased if the change
did not give them good institutions by way of equivalent
for the loss of good possessions, hence it was not to be
endured that democratic innovations should be tolerated
under the shadow of the old flag.   Their indignation,
became contagious.   The Lieutenant-Governor caught it
actively, and shewed that he had done so in the following way :

On opening the Legislature at the " Town of York "

on the 12th October, 1818, Sir Peregrine Maitland said, "Should it appear that a convention of delegates cannot exist without danger to the constitution, in framing a law of prevention, your dispassionate wisdom will be careful that it shall not unwarily trespass on the sacred right of the subject to seek a redress of his grievances by petition." The House of Assembly in their answer assured His Excellency that "we remember that this favoured land was assigned to our fathers as a retreat for suffering loyalty, and not as a sanctuary for sedition." Such a neatly turned sentence could scarcely fail of bearing fruit. Indeed it bore much fruit, for two days afterwards "the dispassionate wisdom" to which His Excellency had appealed, unburdened itself in the following words. The Journals preserve the picturesque resolve which shall be given entire.

"On the motion of MR. JONES, seconded by Mr. VANKOUGHET, it was

"Resolved, that no known member of the meeting of persons styling themselves Delegates from the different Districts of this Province shall be allowed a seat within the bar of this House."

The resolution must have expressed the popular sentiment with tolerable clearness, for it was carried almost unanimously, only two members, Mr. Secord and Mr. Casey, voting "nay." Why the last-named gentlemen were not expelled from the Assembly for giving such an independent vote is not apparent. Surely the occupants of "the retreat" of the true blue type, should have chased away all birds of doubtful plumage from their House, even though they were powerless to effect more stringent measures.

Nothing daunted, however, and in spite of this emphatic expression of "dispassionate wisdom," "Hickory Yankees," "English Luddites," "Scotch Radicals," and "Irish Exiles" continued to flow into "the retreat" disturbing alike the serenity of its atmosphere and the sanctity of its traditions. Unhappily for the "suffering" loyalists the new opinions spread with provoking rapidity, and converts were gained in increasing numbers. The tories were worried and became belligerent. They resented in all directions the utterance of glib speeches and petulant squibs about personal wrongs and popular rights. Besides the classes that felt and complained of political grievances there were the usual number of "Adullamites," generally to be found in all communities, who from one cause or another commonly gravitate towards the party in opposition. Such people are generally unhappy, dislike their neighbours and oppose the government. Thus it may have been that in the same "cave" were mustered, in addition to the political forces proper, all who had wrongs to avenge or slights to remember ; all whose personal aims had been baulked, or whose social ones had been blighted ; all who had missed their rewards, or whose recompense had been unequal to their services ; and all who had laboured towards fixed ends, but whose labours had never borne fruit. These and the like forces being brought into contact very soon lost their individuality. They not only became fused and welded, but naturally took the colour of the largest body. In thus obeying the law of gravitation the party of resistance eventually became the party of reform. Moreover it was this party, made moderate by the many parts of which it was composed, that controlled the constituencies when Lord Sydenham met the Legislature of reunited Canada in the month of June, 1841.

These observations very naturally lead to a second point in the legislation of Canada which is usually regarded as the commencement of our constitutional history. There are passages in the early pages of that history on which Sir Francis Hincks, in his lecture to the St. Patrick's National Association of Montreal, has made some interesting observations, coupled with certain suggestions which deserve examination. It may seem presumptuous to criticize the judgment of one who has sat within the inner circle, and has probably enjoyed the opportunity of looking behind the scenes. Our place, on the contrary, as a spectator has generally been in front of the stage, and not within the " corner " of any of the combatants. But as a bystander we venture to think that the history of the period to which Sir Francis Hincks has referred admits of a different reading from that which he has given it, and the difficulties by which it was marked admit of a fairer solution than the one which Sir Francis Hincks has seen fit to apply.

I

As we have endeavoured to show elsewhere, the privileges of Parliament were claimed and enjoyed by the legislatures of Upper and Lower Canada in spite alike of the law, and in the former case of Dr. Baldwin's opinion to the contrary. It followed that the possessions, no matter how acquired, which the separated legislatures resolved not to part with, were retained with a firm hand by the legislature of the reunited Province· The old question was not again raised. It was settled so to speak by the law of limitation. The trail of 1811 had been carefully covered, and Dr. Baldwin was in no mood to open it in 1841. He kept silence, and wisely, for a new and more ambitious issue was to be raised under the guidance of his conscientious son. No whisper was then heard on the subject of privilege, for it was essential to the work that Mr. Robert Baldwin had in hand that the fiction, which his father had challenged thirty years earlier, should be recognized as a fact, viz., that legislatures were parliaments. Consequently the legislature of Canada being what it was, was entitled not only to enjoy Parliamentary immunities, but also to administer Parliamentary government. The former, as we have seen, under irregular conditions had been forcibly assumed. Might not the latter under favouring circumstances be resolutely acquired? The irregular, not to say spurious, parentage of the proceedings must be kept well in mind if we would understand aright and judge impartially of what subsequently took place.

Suggestions for a system of responsible, or parliamentary government, in different forms and in different places, had frequently been made, but it will generally be admitted that they did not take shape till 1841. Lord Sydenham it is true required his chief departmental officers to find seats in the legislature, but he did so to further his own plans of personal government. They were there to express his views, and to expound his policy, for he had previously complained that members of the Assembly holding office and receiving the pay of the Crown had continually voted against his measures. Whatever opinions Lord Sydenham may have formed on the abstract question of responsible government, it is safe to say that his mode of administering public affairs was controlled by his individual resolve to rule as well as to govern. The resolutions which were agreed to on the 3rd September, 1841, are as follow :

First. "That the Head of the Executive Government of the Province, being within the limits of his Government, the representative of the Sovereign is responsible to the Imperial authority alone ; but that nevertheless the management of our local affairs can only be conducted by him, by and with the assistance, counsel and information of subordinate officers in the Province."

Second. "That in order to preserve between the different branches of the Provincial Parliament that harmony which is essential to the peace, welfare and good government of the Province, the chief advisers of the representative of the Sovereign, constituting a Provincial administration under him, ought to be men possessed of the confidence of the representatives of the people, thus affording a guarantee that the well-understood wishes and interests of the people, which our Gracious Sovereign has declared shall be the rule of the Provincial Government, will, on all occasions, be faithfully represented and advocated."

Third. " That the people of this Province have, moreover, a right to expect from such Provincial Administration the exertion of their best endeavours that the Imperial authority, within its constitutional limits, shall be exercised in the manner most consistent with their well-understood wishes and interests."

These resolutions were cordially agreed to, receiving the almost unanimous assent of the Legislative Assembly. The occasion and the author are remembered throughout the country with honour and affection. For although the resolutions in their amended form are associated in the journals with the name of the late Mr. Harrison, yet all who knew that high-minded gentleman must also be aware, that his keen sense of honour made it impossible that he should wish to appropriate and use as his own either the handiwork, or brain work, of another. Mr. Harrison's name was only accidentally associated with those resolutions. Mr. Baldwin was their true parent. Indeed Mr. Harrison's suggested amendments amounted to little more than grammatical alterations, to which Mr. Baldwin cheerfully assented, playfully adding that, in furtherance of such an important end, " he gladly accepted Lindley Murray as an ally." The principle which those resolutions expressed had previously received the qualified assent of the Earl of Durham, and a nod of approval from a statesman so distinguished was not without advantage to Mr. Baldwin. Unfortunately that self-contained, and self-willed nobleman did much towards neutralizing the value of his mission by petulantly deserting his post and returning to England without leave. However, though he received less rebuke than he deserved, much less than he would have done had he been a person of lower rank and less consideration, he nevertheless had to endure a good deal more than he was very well able to bear. The shadow of the Queen's displeasure, and the frown of the court, were novelties to him, besides he missed what he cared for, the applause and welcome of his countrymen. Less was, consequently, made of his services than those services merited and, less was probably said of his report than would have been the case had he not stained his great trust with political pique and personal insubordination. Nevertheless, his report was generally, if not officially, regarded as an exceedingly valuable narrative, and was especially commended by the mass of colonial reformers who affected liberal opinions.

Returning, however, to Mr. Baldwin's resolutions, and the proceedings from which they should not be separated, we arrive at some important conclusions that are, perhaps, worthy of consideration, and should be kept in view by all who would reach a fair judgment on those points which Sir Francis Hincks has raised as between the colonial office and the Canadian assembly in the matter of Lord Metcalfe's rule, including the instructions by which he was presumably governed and the principles which he endeavoured to carry out.

In the first place it should be borne in mind that Mr. Baldwin's resolutions were nothing more than a declaration of the opinion of the Legislative Assembly. No effort was made to make them express more than the sentiments of the popular branch of the legislature. The Legislative Council was not invited to concur in them, neither were they communicated by address to the Governor General though His Excellency had no doubt previously seen them, and probably had some hand in shaping them to the form they eventually took. Be this as it may they nevertheless halted for the lack of support, as they expressed the opinion of one only, of the three estates of the Canadian legislature ; and even this imperfect opinion, so far as we can discover, was not communicated to the colonial Secretary.

In the second place, Lord Sydenham had received from Lord John Russell, the colonial Secretary, more than one preliminary caution, coupled with a positive instruction as to how the question of responsible government should be dealt with, in the event of its being presented to him in any form whatever. Writing to Lord Sydenham on the 14th October, 1839, Lord John Russell said : " You may encounter much difficulty in subduing ' the excitement which prevails on the question of what is called ' responsible government,' I have to instruct you, however, to refuse any explanation which may be

construed to imply an acquiescence in the petitions and
addresses on this subject." The despatch is too long
to quote in full, but it ends as it commenced with a
caution "against any declaration from which dangerous
consequences might hereafter flow." The lesson, in brief,
evidently was "don't compromise the government, and
keep the prerogative free." The conclusion we draw is,
first, that the concurrent voice of the Canadian legislature was not expressed on the question of "responsible
government;" and, secondly, had the two houses of the
legislature with one voice, and in the same words,
affirmed their resolves, those resolves would have been
incomplete in the absence of the concurrence of His
Excellency the Governor General, as the representative of
the Crown. Such concurrence, however, was neither to
be looked for nor expected, because His Excellency had
previously been instructed by his official superior to do
nothing "that might be construed to imply an acquiescence in the petitions and addresses on the subject."
Therefore, had the resolutions been put into the form of
an address, which they were not, or had they received
the concurrence of the two houses, which they did not,
or had they in any way been officially presented to His
Excellency the Governor General with a request that
they should be transmitted to England, which they were
not, then the case would have presented aspects that it
did not wear, and it might have justified such conclusions
as those which Sir Francis Hincks, as it seems to us,
has somewhat precipitately reached.

Then, again, it is not easy to arrive at a clear idea
of the value that Lord Sydenham attached to "responsible government" as applied to a colony, for his views
on that subject as expressed in 1839 are scarcely in accord with the views expressed for him by his biographer
in 1843. But whatever those views were, we think it
quite certain that His Excellency's standard differed
widely from the standard that Mr. Baldwin had set up.
Both of those eminent men, so to speak, put in a
plea for responsible ministers, but the divergence of
interpretation began as soon as the plea was fyled. Both
were willing to employ the same means, but they were
altogether at variance when they compared the ends
for which those means were to be used; Lord Sydenham
wanted ministers who would represent and express his
personal opinions, while Mr. Baldwin wanted ministers
who would represent and express the opinions of the
people. The former seemed to look at the question
as a handy instrument of executive convenience, while
the latter regarded it as the source of representative
government. Lord Sydenham, perhaps from the force
of circumstances, or from the chronic illiberality that
so frequently lodges in the breasts of liberals, seemed
to think, that government in a colony should of course
be popular, but that its popularity should centre in
the Governor; while Mr. Baldwin, on the other hand,
thought that government should in like manner be
popular, but that its popularity should depend on,

and find its expression in the voice and will of the
people. Now Lord Sydenham in his native land was
a liberal of the liberals, but in Canada, like his predecessor Lord Durham, he is remembered for the imperious qualities of his character, for the despotic fibre
of his will, and for the adroit phases of his rule. He
had unbounded faith in himself and in his plans of
government. Indeed his waverings were not due to
hesitancy or weakness, for he was controlled by neither
one nor the other. When he paused in his plans, it
arose rather from his inability to find suitable instruments to carry them out, than from any doubt of
the soundness of the principles on which they rested.
Actuated by a splendid egotism, he was of too absolute
a nature to consent to aught that would weaken either
his own or the Queen's prerogative. Lord Sydenham was a whig and something more. Like Lord John
Russell, he thoroughly understood how unsatisfactory it
was to attempt to confine principles of government to
exact terms, as well as the extreme hazard of making any
such attempt. Critics no doubt are more adventurous
than statesmen, for the latter generally avoid verbal
definitions when they are required to deal with general
principles. They do not care to place inelastic shackles
either on the functions of the Crown, or on the powers of
the two Houses of Parliament, or indeed on themselves.
They prefer to look at the question of ministerial responsibility as in many respects an open one. We may,

for example, think we know nearly what contingencies should oblige a ministry to resign, but the authorities are by no means agreed as to the time when such resignation should take place. The verdict of the constituencies may suffice for popular conclusions, but as Parliament is the only recognized court of appeal, their contention is not without force who say that a ministry should await the judgment of that court before they act upon the verdict of the constituencies. It has seemed to some authorities as scarcely respectful to such a tribunal as the high court of Parliament, to assume that it is incapable of being impartial ; that it is wholly controlled by foregone conclusions ; that it would decline to hear fresh arguments, and be obstinately unwilling to take a new view of an old case. It fairly may be questioned whether, in the absence of a proper hearing in the proper place, the issue is ripe for judgment. No trial can authoritatively be had, no verdict can officially be rendered, until the whole electorate, in the persons of its representatives, has collectively been appealed to. Parliament should hesitate to abdicate its functions, and pause before it substitutes the individual voice of isolated polling booths for the congregated wisdom of the " grand inquest." The early theory was to listen to the advice of the people as expressed by their representatives in Parliament, and not by a direct appeal, in the nature of a *plebiscitum*, to each voter registered in the electorate. A minister of the Crown is the custodian of his own responsibilities and the fittest judge of his own duties ; and, when not misled by his temper, may safely be trusted to act wisely and in accordance with usage. Usage now points in two directions. Nevertheless a word may be said and a plea put in for the earlier one ; as Parliament does not consist of the House of Commons only. For though it is true that an administration does not now resign in consequence of an adverse vote in the House of Lords, it is also true that such an incident gives a ministry a fearful shaking. Parliament ought not to dissipate its powers, neither should it put its prerogative into commission. That high court was formerly regarded as the place of trial, where a ministry was judged by its peers. To relegate this important duty to the poll booths alone is a decline in usage, and may prove a loss in fact. The late examples in the United Kingdom, and the more recent one in Canada, of ministries resigning on what was accepted as an adverse vote of the constituencies, are so many tributes to the high-mindedness of Mr. Disraeli, of Mr. Gladstone and of Mr. Mackenzie, for they exactly express the course which they, and men like them, might be expected to take in such circumstances. Those gentlemen thought fit, and doubtless with good reason, to assume that they had lost the public confidence, and therefore, in deference to the general convenience, rather than to constitutional usage, they also thought fit to act on the assumption, by declining to be any longer responsible for governing the country.

The question under review, like most questions relating to government, is one that is encompassed with formalities ; and formalities, be it remembered, that are not only crisp with the hoar of experience, but are also valuable securities against the weight of numbers or the oppression of one. Nevertheless the age, whether wisely or not, probably pays as much homage to modern convenience as it does to ancient forms ; but there is danger in such shiftiness, for in our eagerness to lay hold of what is convenient we run grave risk of missing what is best. If a ministry receives nominally from the Sovereign, but actually from Parliament, a charge to do certain things, should it not, irrespective of the question of success or failure, give an account of its doings to the authority from which the charge is received? The question no doubt has two sides. We have presented in part the view that was not adopted. The course that was pursued need not be discussed. The matter is chiefly referred to as illustrative of the wisdom of those statesmen who decline to give exact definitions when dealing with elastic principles. Indeed the most ardent admirers of the British constitution may not like, but cannot help, admitting that it rests on illogical foundations. This fact not infrequently provokes foreigners, because it blocks some favourite theory or destroys some well-constructed argument. Englishmen, on the contrary, have no sympathy with the theoretical disappointments of the most accomplished critits. They are satisfied with their possessions, being well aware that those possessions, however wanting in symmetry, rest on the broad basis of severe experience and established use.

Now, responsible government as applied to a colony was an abstract and untried question, and constitution-alist though he was, Lord John Russell looked at it as one to be avoided. Moreover, he saw that several very critical subjects nestled in its folds, and prominently among them, one of great importance, viz., the Royal prerogative in its relation to the patronage of the Crown. Hence we may conjecture his Lordship earnestly in-structed Lord Sydenham " to do nothing at variance with the honour of the Crown." By way of making the instruction more emphatic, the latter was referred to the resolutions of both Houses of the Imperial Parliament of 1837, which treated of certain speculative questions of Canadian rule and of certain practical ones on the sub-jects of prerogative and patronage. Thus between positive instructions and Parliamentary references Lord Sydenham's conduct, irrespective of his opinions, was put under severe control. Mr. Baldwin was probably aware of the fact, and perhaps also of the peculiarities that governed His Excellency's opinions, and consequently he may not have wished to submit his resolutions to the ordeal of an adverse criticism by causing them to be officially sent to His Excellency. Be this as it may, the important proceedings of that eventful day were supple-mented within the next twenty-four hours by two events, each of which seriously controlled the course of affairs, and probably hastened those changes in the mode of administration for which the public mind in Canada had scarcely been prepared.

Mr. Baldwin's resolutions, judging from the space occupied by the reported proceedings, must have been adopted on the evening of the 3rd September, 1841. On that day, the whig administration under Lord Melbourne was succeeded by Sir Robert Peel, as leader of the conservative party who became for the second time the first Lord of the Treasury, while the late Earl of Derby, then Lord Stanley succeeded Lord John Russell as Secretary of State for the colonies. But the change of ministry in England would probably not have seriously affected the administration of affairs in Canada had it not been accompanied by a local calamity of a very serious kind. On the following day, viz., 4th September, 1841, when taking his usual afternoon ride, Lord Sydenham's horse suddenly fell, causing such complicated fractures, and other acute injuries to the rider, as to result in his comparatively early death a fortnight later. Thus, at a most critical juncture in our history, when standing on the threshold of a new career, and not knowing whether Parliamentary government in Canada, being so crudely introduced, would be conceded or not, two apparently untoward events took place. There was a change of ministry in England, and, for all practical purposes, there was a collapse of the government of Canada. For it should be remembered that Lord Sydenham was no ordinary Governor, and the period of his rule was a time of transition from a mode of administration that the country had outgrown, to another form of government which was only in a process of taking shape. Lord Sydenham was the grand figure of this transition period, for he really seemed to be.

"Lord of himself and all beside."

He was not only the Governor General and the chief of the local administration, but practically he was the leader and whipper-in of the government in the legislature. He soothed the refractory with fair speeches and allowed honours to dangle before the eyes of the ambitious. Trade and commerce, finance and banking he took naturally to as a matter of course, for they were parts of his political heritage; but foreign affairs and matters of local self-government were subjects on which he was by no means inclined to be silent or to affect indifference. All he wanted appeared to be suitable instruments, men who would obey his orders and who possessed the skill to develope his plans. Ministers in his day, like silver in the time of Solomon, "were nothing accounted of." His judgment was the crucible to which all subjects were to be brought, and his mind the channel through which all opinions were to find expression. But, alas! the clear head and the firm hand, though they achieved much, could not resist the inevitable. They surrendered in company, and now rest within the walls of the old parish church at Kingston.

The two events just referred to should be kept in mind, for the derangements in Canadian affairs that almost immediately took place, and to which Sir Francis Hincks has made particular allusion, may be, and we incline to think are, due to the meeting together of those important occurrences, viz., the sudden change of the ministry in England and the sudden death of the Governor in Canada. It will also bear repeating that the resolutions expressed the opinions of the Legislative Assembly only. Mr. Baldwin may have doubted whether the Legislative Council would agree to them, and silence in that case was wiser than a conflict of opinion. It certainly would have been impolitic to bid for a negative. Besides. being on his death-bed, the Governor General was tied by his instructions, and could scarcely have returned a colourless answer to such an important communication. In the language of Lord John Russell's despatch he might have said "that he was bound by his instructions to refuse any explanation which might be construed to imply an acquiescence in the petitions and addresses on this subject." Moreover, His Excellency's opinion would be read and criticised by people in the mother country who would not trouble themselves to look at the question out of which it arose. Thus Mr. Baldwin kept his treasure intact. He neither exposed it to the chilling resistance of the Legislative Council nor to the official condemnation of the Governor General. Having honestly acquired for his resolutions the affirmation of the body whose opinion he most valued, he determined to keep those resolutions undisturbed till the time should arrive when they could be appealed to with advantage, and put into force with the consent of all the estates of the legislature.

In the meanwhile the subject was hampered by incomplete arrangements, and perhaps hindered by the obligations of official routine. The votes and proceedings at that time were not, as they now are, printed daily for the use of members. The newspapers were not as generous then as they now are in supplying reports of legislative proceedings, and the manuscript breviates of routine matters, furnished to His Excellency under the direction of the clerks of the two Houses, were more remarkable for conciseness than for fullness of detail. So far as we have been able to discover there is no evidence to show that those resolutions were sent to the Governor General, or were forwarded to the colonial Secretary, or formed one of the miscellaneous collection of state documents that in the Imperial Parliament are grouped under the head of " Canada Papers." As neither resolutions nor address were to be found in the Governor General's office, Sir Richard Jackson, Lord Sydenham's interim successor, may fairly be excused if he failed to make any communication on the subject to the colonial Secretary,

K

for the routine method of sending copies, when pub-
lished, of the journals of the two Houses to England can
scarcely be regarded as a special communication.   Sir
Francis Hincks may have had access to sources of information not within our reach, and they may have force
sufficient to overthrow our hypothetical fabric.   Our
findings are so meagre and unsatisfactory as to press home
the conclusion that the colonial Secretary was scarcely
aware of the existence of such resolutions, until the fact
was suddenly brought to his knowledge by the appearance in his presence of the first victim to the new principles which those resolutions expressed.   The reflections
to which such an incident must have given rise were alike
new and inconvenient.   The Imperial authority had
been wholly set aside ; for questions of prerogative had
been dealt with irrespective of all reference to the source
of prerogative.   A declaration of opinion by one branch
of a colonial legislature had suddenly been substituted
for the earlier, and till then the recognized procedure as
the rule of government, and the Queen's representative,
apparently without authority, and in spite of instructions
to the contrary, had accepted the substitution.   As a
consequence, the Queen's government found themselves
in a maze of grievances which they had no part in bringing about, but which they were required peremptorily to
redress.   Intelligence arrived with unpleasant rapidity.
The stereotyped story of a breach of faith though articulated by new voices was told in the old words.   The

vision of a crowd of colonial officials "whose services had been dispensed with" was too disquieting to be meekly borne. A colonial Governor had acted without authority, and by exceeding his instructions had laid on the colonial Secretary duties beyond his power to discharge. There must be a check to, if not a reversal of, such a system of rule, and a Governor was required who would prove equal to the occasion. A state of ignorance had been for too long a time continued, but as it was fairly excusable, it should not have occasioned surprise. Accident had been a powerful factor, while change and indifference had been skilful allies. The three influences had successfully, by strange misadventures, combined to intercept knowledge and divert attention from matters that were nevertheless urgent. The concurrence at the same time of the death of Lord Sydenham, of the resignation of the whig ministry, and of the interregnum in the government of Canada, represented disturbing elements of a very active kind. Lord Sydenham died before the information reached Canada that Lord John Russell had been succeeded by Lord Stanley at the colonial office. What might have chanced had his life been prolonged it were idle to conjecture. Important communications in due time would have been made, and the colonial Secretary apprized of the drift that had set in towards Parliamentary government. Nevertheless the crisis had not actually arisen. Lord Sydenham's ministers remained in office, for the period was the mid-

summer vacation, and hence they were not disquieted by the sessional worries of an unconfiding legislature.
But such a paradise of peace could only last for a short
time. The season of crisis drew rapidly near. Unhappily the Queen's interim representative was not supposed
to be much interested in, or acquainted with, our colonial
politics, so that he scarcely felt called upon to note their
character and tendency. The commander of the forces,
Sir Richard Jackson, on whom the administration of the
Government devolved on the death of Lord Sydenham,
was a soldier rather than a statesman, and, consequently,
the precision which usually attaches to the former character would be observed in the mode of transacting his
civil duties. We may assume that Sir Richard read his
orders and obeyed them. He sent to the colonial Secretary what he was required to send, and he abstained from
discussing what he was not called on to consider. As
the Assembly had expressed no wish to send Mr. Baldwin's resolutions to the colonial Secretary, why should
they be sent? Being the opinions of one branch of the
legislature only, they were incomplete utterances, and
without any force of law. Why trouble the Secretary with
crude and imperfect papers? If such were the facts, Sir
Richard Jackson may fairly have thought that his duty
was best discharged by attending only to such matters as
lay within his reach, or in regard to which some desire
had been generally expressed that he should perform
them. Such seems to have been the state of affairs

between September, 1841, and February, 1842, when the administrator, Sir Richard Jackson, was relieved of his duties by the arrival of the new governor general, the Right Honourable Sir Charles Bagot.

Then the dormant life of Mr. Baldwin's resolutions suddenly became active, and the awaking was followed by much whispering and many surprises. What had theretofore been regarded as an abstract proposition possessing only a theoretical value, was found to be an active principle seething with practical force. What were once merely declarations of opinion not only became rules of conduct, but were, ere long, and in various uncomfortable ways, destined to be borne into the inner chambers of the colonial office. Moreover they were of sufficient importance to arrest attention, for they represented Imperial as well as Colonial issues They included a change in old usages, a departure from old traditions, and a reversal of received opinions. The order of the colonial service was challenged, and its discipline was to be placed under colonial control. " Powers, privileges and immunities " had violently been retained, and now patronage and prerogative were to be boldly appropriated. The time had come for authority to speak, for strange truths were being brought home, accompanied with interpretations that were exceedingly disturbing. Moreover such revelations were made, not by a dainty process of patient endeavour, but by means of a rude shock and a breach in the wall. New bearings had to be taken to suit the new era, for evidently the point of a fresh departure had been reached. The question clamoured for settlement, whether the new way should be followed or the old one persevered in. Lord Stanley was officially required to examine the policy which Sir Charles Bagot had pursued and the course he had taken. He was required to see whether it was complete in itself and whether it was in harmony with the royal instructions. Such an inquiry having presumably been made, the result must have disclosed two facts, and suggested one conclusion. The facts being that the resolutions expressed only the opinions of one branch of the Canada legislature, and that those opinions were inconsistent with the positive instructions that Lord John Russell, the immediate predecessor of Lord Stanley in office, had sent to Lord Sydenham. The conclusion arrived at, in all probability, was that Mr. Baldwin's resolutions were not only inconsistent with English policy, but that they were directly opposed to ministerial orders. Nevertheless, the issue raised would scarcely have ruffled the equanimity of Downing Street had it not been pointed with injustice as well as inconvenience; but such were the facts. The abstract question was made to fit into a personal one, in respect of which the subject of a very serious colonial wrong had the advantage of the counsel and aid of a learned and very influential imperial ally. Thus, the resisting forces, besides being well placed, were able and energetic, having, moreover, a backing of sufficient strength to command the attention of colonial office officials. Parliamentary privileges, by dint of perseverance, had practically been retained by the local legislatures, in spite of cautions from England and of remonstrance in Canada. Indeed remonstrance had been destroyed by the heat with which it was encountered, and hence no second occasion had arisen for reviewing the judgment of the legislature, or for challenging the decision of the courts. Silence, thenceforward, became the best security. In like manner Parliamentary government would, in all probability, not only have been cheerfully conceded, but garnished with compliments, had not its introduction been attended with entangling conditions, official inconveniences and personal ill-usage. Unfortunately the theoretical question was compromised by the practical one, for it encouraged men to think, and not unnaturally, that a system whose introduction was attended with wrong to individuals could scarcely be worked with benefit to the community. There can be little doubt that responsible government in Canada was blemished on the threshold of its history by an act of injustice. The incident, moreover, threatened to become an example that might be followed in other places with exact, or perhaps aggravated, imitations. The narrative to which we shall refer, included an ugly passage that not only touched the honour of the Sovereign, but threatened the colonial office with critical difficulties, for, while it altered the conditions of service, it practically changed the source of patronage, and, above all, it menaced the authorities at Downing Street with the untiring importunities of placemen out of place.

By means of a special council of his own selection, Lord Sydenham had succeeded in governing Lower Canada, but he had made no approach whatever towards conciliating the good-will of Her Majesty's subjects of French origin.   He managed to get through the first session of the legislature of United Canada with the help only of ministers of the English-speaking race, but the way was alike hard and indefensible to him and them. It was therefore most undesirable that the strategy of the first session should be repeated in the second, and perhaps no one better than Lord Sydenham knew that any such attempt would result in failure.   The time for continuing an irritating and exclusive policy could not be indefinitely prolonged, but, until the arrival of the new Governor General, there seemed to be no one with authority sufficient to initiate a fairer and wiser rule. Such was the state of affairs when Sir Charles Bagot arrived at Kingston on the 12th January, 1842.   The ministers that his predecessor had bequeathed to him were eight gentlemen, all of whom were of the English-speaking race.   With them it would be his duty to take counsel, for the act would have been deemed unconstitutional had he sought advice beyond the privileged circle of his sworn advisers.   The difficulties of the situation were clearly seen by Sir Charles Bagot, who made some ineffectual attempts to overcome them. Although the aim of his effort was appreciated, the mode did not find favour with the class in whose interests it was made. Matters moved on unsatisfactorily and with increasing friction till the 8th of September, when the Legislature met " for the despatch of business." Having the opportunity, and acting within the limits of its supposed authority, the Legislative Assembly lost no time in recording its opinions on several important subjects. Mr. Baldwin, for example, seconded by Mr. Barthe, availed himself of his constitutional right to move an amendment to the address in answer to the speech from the throne, in which amendment the principle enunciated in the resolutions on responsible government of the former session was reaffirmed. It was declared that the " chief advisers of His Excellency constituting the provincial administration under him should be men possessed of the confidence of the representatives of the people," adding, by way of illustrating his meaning, that such "confidence is not reposed in His Excellency's present advisers." The amended address no doubt would have passed had not Sir Charles Bagot anticipated the obligation, which the adoption of that amendment would have laid on him, by sending for Mr. Lafontaine. The interview led to a correspondence that resulted in the retirement of messieurs Draper, Ogden, and Sherwood from the administration, and to the substitution of messieurs Lafontaine and Baldwin in their stead. The conciliation of "our fellow subjects who are of French origin" was a very satisfactory feature of the new start, and found expression in the emphatic words of a resolution, which, on the motion of Mr. Dunscomb, seconded by Mr. Simpson, was adopted almost unanimously by the Legislative Assembly, only five members voting "nay."

The correspondence between Sir Charles Bagot and Mr. Lafontaine on that important occasion is very interesting and instructive. Though no reference was made in terms to the question of responsible government, it nevertheless led to the observance of those conditions on which the principle is supposed to rest ; for a provincial administration was formed, with His Excellency's sanction, of "men possessed of the confidence of the representatives of the people." In his effort to redress the wrongs of a race, His Excellency practically established that system of constitutional government which Mr. Robert Baldwin had advocated, and to which he had given expression in his celebrated resolutions. It is nevertheless important to bear in mind the distinction between what His Excellency did and what he intended to do, for there is nothing in his letter to show that the radical changes to which it immediately led were present to his mind. His Excellency's sole aim appeared to be to gain the good will of, and to do justice to, "the population of French origin," and this was accomplished

without direct references to any abstract question of
government. Unfortunately, the work of redressing
wrongs was not accomplished without creating wrongs.
No doubt the class irritation that culminated in the
troubles of 1837–8 had scarcely subsided. Passion,
when quickened by revolt and coloured with blood, does
not cool suddenly, nevertheless it can scarcely be questioned that the relief of a race which had been slighted
and overlooked would have been more wisely obtained
had it not have been accompanied by injuries done to
individuals of another race who were guiltless of wrong.
In his laudable endeavour to effect the object that Mr.
Lafontaine had at heart, His Excellency assented to
the sacrifice of an official whose interests he was especially bound to protect. The act was more than a blun-
der, for if it did not show what responsible government
meant, it taught by an ugly example what responsible
government would include and might effect. The lesson
was not lost in England. On the contrary it apparently
made a great impression there, and for a time not only
disquieted the colonial office but arrested the course of
constitutional government in Canada.

Sir Charles Bagot had not been a member of the
House of Commons, and personally was unacquainted
with the duties of a cabinet minister. Nevertheless his
experiences as a diplomatist must have been valuable,
for they probably qualified him to assay character, to
overcome differences, to conciliate enmities, and to

draw together those who had been estranged. To a mind thus educated, and to habits thus acquired, were added great colloquial gifts, and a superb presence, for Sir Charles Bagot was a grand specimen of manly beauty. Thus equipped by nature, education, and experience the new Governor was by no means ill prepared to face the difficulties that met him on his arrival at Kingston. There was method, too, in his mode of going to work. Lord John Russell's instructions to Lord Sydenham on the subject of responsible government, it should be remembered, were not cancelled by reason of the change of the English administration, neither could Sir Charles Bagot recognize as law the resolutions of one branch only of the law-making power. His Excellency appears carefully to have avoided the discredited expression " responsible government," for those words have no place in his letter. Of course he was not the man deliberately to violate his instructions, for the instinct of obedience in his case had not only been cultivated by experience, but was a habit of his life. Nevertheless his agreement with Mr. Lafontaine included the exact conditions which Mr. Baldwin had endeavoured to enforce, and against the adoption of which Canadian Governors had been more than once cautioned. Local criticism may have shed unwelcome light on His Excellency's act, enabling him perchance to see by the interpretation put on it that he had really overstepped the limit of his instructions, and had wandered into forbidden paths. The correspondence between the colonial Secretary and himself, to which the act gave rise, could have been known only to few, and was no doubt confidential in its character. That it included some expressions of surprise as to the course that had been pursued is probable enough, and it may have been that these recollections and other trials lodging in his mind prompted his dying injunction to those around him "to defend his memory." His wish has been abundantly respected in Canada, and by none more reverently than by the "inhabitants of French origin" whom he served so faithfully.

On his arrival in Canada Sir Charles Bagot must have felt, what everybody said, that "the peace, welfare and good government of the country" could only be carried on by the hearty co-operation of the English and French speaking peoples. There was no difference of opinion on this point, but as the latter had stood resolutely aloof, it became the duty of His Excellency to inquire the reason, and then smooth the way to such an alliance between the races as would make government not only possible but satisfactory. Whereupon His Excellency sent for the head and representative of the French Canadian party, and put himself into official communication with him. Thus arose the correspondence between Sir Charles Bagot and Mr. Lafontaine. It soon became clear that nothing could be done without the aid of the latter, and it therefore was necessary to inquire on what terms his assistance could be obtained. The answer will be found in the memorable correspondence of the 13th and 16th September, 1842. It is too long for quotation in full, but there are three points to which it is necessary to refer, and these must be kept steadily in mind if we desire to possess the key to those events that subsequently occurred.

A way had to be found for the introduction into the executive council of certain gentlemen of French origin, who should represent the majority in Lower Canada, and to this end vacancies had to be forcibly made, and, the incumbents had, in the interests of public policy, to be relieved and set at large. The office of Attorney General for Lower Canada was one of those which Mr. Lafontaine required to be vacated. But in assenting to this condition, and in assigning the succession to the last-named gentleman, Sir Charles Bagot caused it to be distinctly understood " that provision should be made for Mr. Ogden commensurate with his long and faithful services." The like condition was attached to the case of Mr. Davidson.

In his answer Mr. Lafontaine fell in with the views that had been expressed by Sir Charles Bagot, adding, however, an important qualification with respect to Messrs. Ogden and Davidson in the following words : " That the proposition to make provision for the retiring officers, Mr. Ogden and Mr. Davidson, be considered an open question." This modification, which was a mistake alike in policy and in justice, received His Excellency's assent. Thus it was that Sir Charles Bagot assisted at the deprivation of an officer whose commission like his own was derived from the Crown, with this difference, however, that the condition of service in the case of the Attorney General was expressed originally in the words " during good behaviour," and in the case of a Governor in the words " during pleasure." Thus His Excellency fell into the error of exchanging an absolute for a conditional security. In a moment of high-minded trustfulness, His Excellency parted with the control of the case, and left to the action of an unfriendly Legislature the interests of a public servant whom he was bound to protect. The misfortune was aggravated by the fact that Mr. Ogden was then absent from Canada on leave, and could not therefore personally defend his rights. The transaction was easily epitomized. " In the interests of public policy His Excellency was constrained to sacrifice a public servant." This kind of offering is occasionally necessary, but the sacrifice ought not to be aggravated by unmerited suffering. His Excellency was evidently of this opinion, but he had rendered himself powerless, and the discovery was made only too late. In less than three weeks afterwards he tried to recover what he had lost, but found to his sorrow his effort end in failure. He had, at Mr. Lafontaine's request, consented to the question of remunerating Messrs. Ogden and Davidson being left an open one, but when he sent his message on the 3rd of October his recommendation was evaded and postponed. No motion for consideration followed the reading, and when nine days afterwards Mr. Hincks, seconded by Mr. Harrison, moved that the message be considered, he was tripped by an amendment, which was carried in a House of fifty members by a majority of twenty, that the consideration be postponed to a future Session. It may here be added that the indicated session arrived, but the subject was not revived. Sir Charles Bagot had died, and Mr. Ogden had carried his complaint to England.

Mr. Ogden had reason to think that he had fallen a victim to conflicting views. His Excellency the Governor General on one hand, and the Legislative Assembly on the other, had looked at his claims from opposite points, and had arrived at opposite conclusions. The postponement of the consideration of a question so simple in itself, and at the same time so serious to His Excellency and to the subject of it, admitted only of one interpretation. Wherefore Mr. Ogden took his course, turned his back on the Legislature of his native country, and determined to see whether he could obtain in England the justice that had eluded him in Canada. The state of parties in the mother country favoured his application, for Lord Lyndhurst, his near connection, if not a relative, was the Lord Chancellor at that time. Mr. Ogden knew well that his case would be considered by his kinsman, and he knew further that that kinsman was credited with the keenest intellect in England. The case was prepared with the greatest care, for law and rhetoric contributed to make it perfect. It was then severely reviewed by friends in Canada, and when stripped of all redundancy, and every point sharpened by the action of wisdom and temper, it was finally copied and sent home. Lord Lyndhurst gave his friendly and sympathetic thought to the narrative, and by appointing the subject of it to the office of Attorney General for the Isle of Man plainly shewed that, in being displaced from his situation in Canada without compensation or equivalent, Mr. Ogden had not forfeited his claim to the consideration of the crown.

How the whole question was viewed by Lord Lyndhurst has not been disclosed, neither is it known to what extent Lord Stanley's views may have been influenced by the opinion of his colleague. It is not difficult to believe that Lord Lyndhurst saw as clearly as Mr. Baldwin that "responsible government" had been conceded in fact if not in words, and that, as a consequence of the concession, the prerogative of the crown had, so to speak, been put into commission, and that thenceforward, unless the evil could be stayed, patronage could only be exercised in the colonies in deference to the will of a provincial administration, composed of men possessing the confidence of the representatives of the people. Thus the condition against which successive Governors had been cautioned actually arose. The new theory of colonial government had been practically explained by an example, and the illustration and the man were alike within reach. It was not, it may be admitted, wise to introduce the new reform in a raiment of wrong, and furnish a gentleman of clear intellect and high character with a grievance of almost startling force. Such an introduction would prove in the last degree damaging in Downing street. Mr. Hincks and Mr. Harrison wisely sought to avert the evil, but they failed, and the reform party suffered in their failure, for it is by no means improbable that the wretched struggles of the next seven years were more or less due to the doubts that arose, and to the irritation that was occasioned by the evasion of the Legislative Assembly to make a suitable provision for Mr. Ogden in 1842. People who scarcely trouble themselves to examine abstract principles becomes exceedingly sensitive when brought face to face with actual examples.

It must be borne in mind that the rights of the Crown had been touched without leave, for while the colonial office had hazy views on the subject of " responsible government," it held clear ones on the subject of patronage. The latter had been assailed, and the assault reverberated as a note of alarm in every corridor of the colonial service. It was easy to see that compassion would block preferment, and the recognition of old claims would stand in the way of new candidates.

Thus a noxious vision of " returned empties " floated before the minds of an army of eligibles who were eagerly waiting for vacant robes or earnestly looking for knightly ribbands. " Responsible government " had previously been approached on all sides, but it had also been uniformly declined by colonial secretaries and persistently discredited by colonial governors. Now, however, it was examined by a new class of investigators, and condemned, without doubt, as a horrible invention, opposed alike to the prerogative of the crown as well as to the reversionary interests of those who were candidates for royal favours. For different reasons the Colonial Secretary found himself surrounded by large numbers of interested critics who had motives in common for preventing the spread of the new heresy, while he, on his part, was immediately concerned in limiting the number of crown beneficiaries and of getting rid altogether of visitors from the colonies burdened with grievances.

The conclusion suggested by these speculative considerations is not far to seek. Had no personal issue, consequent on a disturbing act of injustice, been raised ; had Mr. Ogden been disburdened of his grievance when he was deprived of his office, it is probable that parliamentary government, like parliamentary privilege, though irregularly acquired, and doubtfully exercised, would have become without noise or violence one of the smooth fittings of the Canadian constitution. Had not Mr. Ogden been armed with a grievance, sharpened by a loss which Lord Lyndhurst regarded as a wrong, it is most probable that the course of our history would have flowed onwards undisturbed by Lord Stanley's constitutional heat, or Lord Metcalfe's paternal philosophy. The theoretical disquiet of that period would not have arisen. The alarm of authority would not have been experienced. The talks between Lords Stanley and Metcalfe would have occasioned no anxiety. The meaning of "responsible government," as we now understand it, would never have been challenged, and the literary torture to which the words were exposed under the rule of Lord Metcalfe would not have occurred. The Lafontaine-Baldwin administration of 1842 would not have been relieved of office in 1843, nor, we venture to think, would the new principle of parliamentary government have been subjected to a baptism of fire in 1849. Mischief and misery are the common fruits of individual wrong and personal injustice ; for if there is sweeetness, there is also danger in revenge. Torture not unfrequently gives strength to weakness, and men are surprised at the blow which an injured person can infliet. Had Mr. Hincks and Mr. Harrison succeeded in preventing a case being made for counsel, and sueh a counsel as Lord Lyndhurst in 1842, no occasion, we believe, would have arisen either for the criticism of Sir Francis Hincks on what must be regarded as an obscure and unsatisfactory passage of our history, or for our adventure in suggesting a new reading of an old story.

" Are Legislatures Parliaments ? " The question again arises, and suggests a historical parallel. As in 1792 His Excellency Governor Simcoe, without any authority that has been shown, saw fit, in words at all events, to graft the powers, privileges, and immunities of the parliament of the United Kingdom on the legislature of Upper Canada, so also in 1842, His Excellency Sir Charles Bagot, in the face of instructions to previous governors, saw fit to graft, in fact if not in words, the system of parliamentary government that obtains in England on the system of legislative rule that was provided for Canada. The boons thus bestowed were in excess of the authority of the givers, and both, it is believed, became subjects of correspondence by successive colonial secretaries. One was passively and without much resistance retained, but the other was only acquired after a violent and prolonged struggle. Now, however, parliamentary privilege together with parliamentary government have passed into the undisputed possession of the Parliament of Canada, for the terms of their conveyance are distinctly stated in an act of the Parliament of the United Kingdom. Henceforward no one will question the worth of those possessions, for they bear the sterling marks, and were granted only to the supreme legislature of Canada. They were the growth of experience as well as of controversy, not only in spite of, but through difficulties and oppositions that seemed altogether insurmountable. The words appear equally applicable to states as to persons :

" There's a Divinity that shapes our ends,
Rough hew them as we will."

Though separated by an interval of fifty years, Governor Simcoe and Sir Charles Bagot seem to have been alike desirous of raising the local legislatures to the highest rank, and to this end to clothe them with the attributes of parliament. Those eminent men, with the intuition of statesmen, apparently saw, though afar off, to what authority those limited inquests would eventually grow, and hence they did not hesitate by word and deed to promote as far as in them lay whatever was best suited to advance and strengthen such growth. We are witnesses of what has taken place, and if we are wise we shall contentedly appreciate the greater freedom our political institutions have acquired, and the fuller consideration we have consequently won. In passing, it may be noted that Governor Simcoe and Sir Charles Bagot were of the same political school, and held sympathetic opinions of the value to the empire of " ships, colonies and commerce." They were both tories. Both were large-hearted and open-handed rulers. They withheld nothing it was in their power to grant, and even when, under the guidance of an attractive illusion, they professed to bestow what they had not the right to give, the intention betrayed a generous and far-seeing purpose, for its aim was to promote the happeness of the Canadian people and not to advance the private or selfish ends of their rulers. Superfine cynics say of such persons, and of others like minded, that they belong to the " stupid party." It would be easy to exchange sneer for sneer, and answer such imputations in words conveniently chosen from the vocabulary of scorn. But it is not necessary, for, were the reproach true, it would not change the fact that Canada is as much and many think more indebted to the party thus defamed than to the party of its defamers for the most valuable, and the most enduring parts in her system of constitutional government.

CHAPTER VI.

ALTHOUGH the principle of responsible or parliamentary government had been accepted as a dogma and placed among the verities of government by its conscientious author, as well as by other professors of the same political faith, it was not as thoroughly liked by less advanced students who had not been educated in the same school. They regarded the novelty with suspicion, and did not trouble themselves to appreciate what they made little effort to understand. In the minds of such persons opinion had not taken an exact or trustworthy form, for it had neither been hardened by observation, nor rounded by experience. The subject, no doubt, received much attention from ardent politicians of the professional type, but it was scarcely appreciated by less ambitious people—and such persons represent the majority in most communities, for the indifferent classes, if less influential, are generally more numerous than the active ones. Indeed, lovers of quiet regarded the new tenet as a menace to their peace, and assailed it chiefly because they thought it would create enmities and encourage disturbance. Some were of opinion that the experiment would disagree with the country, and did not like to try what threatened to be injurious. Others, again, caricatured the advocates of the new doctrine, and assailed them with gibes and epigrams, as if their theory of government were not only a crudity to be examined but a jest to be laughed at. All, however, agreed that the latest article of political faith could not be accepted as final or complete, because it it was the confession of one branch only of the Provincial Legislature. Thus, on the very threshold of its career, and apart from the question whether parliamentary government could properly be grafted on a legislature that had not been promoted to the dignity of a parliament, the new deliverance was subjected to the common ordeal of critical examination, sharp discussion and suspicious resistance.

Nor was it in the provinces only that people doubted and looked askance. The authorities at Downing street cordially sympathized with Her Majesty's sceptical subjects in Canada, and evidently discouraged what colonial governors had frequently been instructed to resist. No doubt, in the period of his administration, Lord Sydenham had played with the subject, but it was not to fondle it as a lover, but rather to discredit it with his doubts, if not to mock it with his scorn, that he stooped to examine it. For, whatever Lord Sydenham's views may have been on the abstract question, they were exceedingly unlike, if not absolutely contrary, to those of Mr. Baldwin. Indeed, they were more in harmony with the opinions afterwards expressed by Lord Metcalf; for both of those noblemen agreed that their ministers were

to be responsible to them and not to the people, and
they were to be consulted only when their advice was
required.   Lord Sydenham apparently did not entertain
very exalted views of the provincial legislatures, and,
consequently had no encouraging words at command
when he described their way of doing ordinary work.
It was, therefore, no part of his endeavour to increase
the actual powers or to heighten the assumed importance
of legislative bodies that, even in their subordinate places,
had not only made themselves troublesome, but had
evinced an uncomfortable disposition to become aggres-
sive.   Nevertheless, had the Parliament of the United
Kingdom previously enacted that the legislatures of
British North America should respectively be composed
of " The Queen, an Upper House, styled the Legislative
Council and a Lower one, styled the House of Assembly,"
and had it furthermore declared that such organizations should be parliaments, it is probable that His
Excellency would not have treated the question of responsible government as one foreign to the bodies to
which it had been applied, neither would he have made
it, in its enlarged form, a mark against which to direct
his cynical observations ; as, for example, when he wrote,
" I have already done much to put it down in its inad-
missible sense, namely, the demand that the council
shall be responsible to the assembly, and that the
Governor   shall   take   their   advice   and   be   bound
by it."   *   *   *   "They   are   a   council   for   the

Governor to consult, and nothing more." In His Excellency's opinion, they were a council responsible to him and not to the people; to be the exponents of his views and not of theirs whom they had been chosen to represent. Moreover they were expected so to influence the two houses of the legislature as to secure support for His Excellency's policy and the passage of His Excellency's measures. In short, they were to be used only when His Excellency required their services, to receive instructions rather than to offer advice, and to be active in the assembly but reticent in the cabinet. Thus, in one way and another, by skilful tactics and the adroit use of familiar weapons, Lord Sydenham succeeded in scrambling through the first session of the legislature of re-united Canada. This was all, it should be added, that he had proposed to himself, all that his health enabled him to accomplish. But a period of a painful kind, one quite beyond his reckoning, was put in another form to his work, for all his plans were baulked by his early death. Whether His Excellency should not have commenced the new career in a more conciliatory and considerate temper it were idle to inquire. He made the fact tolerably clear that, in his opinion, it was only a legislature of limited responsibilities and inferior rank that he had to deal with, and that, therefore, it was only entitled to his qualified consideration. He had obeyed his instructions, and had neither entertained memorial nor petition having for their object the enlargement of the powers, or the increase of the responsibilities, of colonial government. He had done his part in starting the newly constituted legislature; but he had done nothing, nor did he wish to do anything, towards raising that legislature to the rank and dignity of a parliament. As he had made it, so he left it, a legislature and nothing more.

When the end of the session arrived, thoughtful persons, irrespective of party bias, began to reflect on the blemishes by which it had been marked. Many of them recalled with unfeigned regret the irritating election tricks and unworthy contrivances that had preceded that session, as well as the uncomfortable antagonism that had been maintained between the English and French speaking races. Thus it chanced that hope became heavy laden and looked inquiringly into the future; for it seemed as if the new vessel was stranded as soon as she was launched. Sir Charles Bagot, Lord Sydenham's immediate successor, had no sooner examined the difficulties which he had inherited, than he found himself obliged seriously to qualify, if not absolutely to reverse, Lord Sydenham's policy, and to assume with Mr. Baldwin, not only that the Canada legislature was a parliament, but that, being a parliament, it should enjoy parliamentary government. Perhaps in his generosity of thought Sir Charles Bagot was incautious, and went further than he had authority to go, and possibly conceded more than he had a right to grant. Practically he acted on a settlement that lacked signatures and seals, that was inconsis-

tent with the instructions which his predecessor had received, and presumably with the brief which he had especially been retained to hold. Without, as we venture to
think, any sufficient warrant, Sir Charles Bagot anticipated by twenty-five years the action of the Parliament of
the United Kingdom when all doubts were removed, for,
by giving effect to Mr. Baldwin's resolutions, he partially
clothed in 1842 the legislature of the re-united provinces with the prerogatives and powers that were only
perfectly conferred in 1867, when the " Parliament of
Canada " was established under the authority of the
British North America Act.

His Excellency's proceedings occasioned much criticism in Canada, but there is reason to think that the
authorities at Downing street were even more disturbed
by what had taken place. The new way of governing
colonies must have suggested many difficulties, for it
seemed to include an inconvenient usurpation of the
royal prerogative. Nor was the outlook improved by
the consideration that the new and large powers had
been appropriated and used without the authority of the
Imperial Parliament. People anxiously inquired whither
such a policy would lead, and whom it would strike.
The Downing street atmosphere was unsettled and
laden with disturbances. Squalls from the provinces
threatened the authorities at home, while abasement in
various shapes seemed to menace the public servants
abroad. But, to make matters worse, not only was the

new way precipitous and alarming, but he who began to travel on it had been taken ill, and was in danger.   The crisis was serious, for not only was the pilot disabled, but the owners were unacquainted with the chart by which he had been steering.   However, they appeared to think that two duties were at once to be discharged. One was to recover the old method of colonial management, and the other was to send out a successor to Sir Charles Bagot who would prove equal to the duty of making the recovery.   They lost no time in accomplishing the latter, but how the former was attempted we shall see presently.

Though a liberal and something more in his relation to English politics, Lord Metcalfe had the reputation of being a skilful administrator, which all liberals are not, and a blameless representative of personal government, which few persons, whether liberals or tories, have enough ballast and calmness successfully to be.   He was, there is reason to believe, among other reasons, chosen to repair the mistake that Sir Charles Bagot had made, or was supposed to have made, and if such were the fact, perhaps no fitter instrument could have been found to accomplish the work, assuming, of course, that such work was worthy of accomplishment, and was within the reach of administrative capability.   Lord Metcalfe had a large heart, a strong will and an open hand.   He was high minded, clear headed and benevolent.   His cheques appeared to be made upon an inexhaustible exchequer, for apparently he was unable to overdraw his account. Whatever the object, the contribution was gracefully offered as if the donor thought that charity should always be censed with sweetness and wrapped in smiles. It might, we think, be truly said of him not only that he never turned his back on any poor man, but that he never closed his purse to any worthy object. His Lordship, no doubt, had been accustomed to rule, but it had been his practice to do so in a fatherly way, for, bachelor though he was, he appeared to think no form of government was better than a fatherly one. Nor can there be any doubt that such opinion is well founded, provided always that the theory is illustrated by such examples as were supplied in Lord Metcalfe's person and manner of life. Unfortunately these qualities are not usually found in alliance, for there are people, and unfortunately their name is legion, who are familiar enough with the despotism that never heard of, much less experienced, the paternity.

But, to return to our subject, it may well be doubted whether Mr. Baldwin's resolutions were actually present to Sir Charles Bagot's thoughts at the time he gave them practical effect. It was His Excellency's duty to carry on the Queen's government, and he desired to do so by and with the assistance of all the Queen's subjects. The Canadians of French origin had till then retired within their own lines, and consequently had stood aloof. They had reason for doing so, for, having been slighted and treated as unworthy alike of confidence or favour, they felt aggrieved and were resentful. It was, therefore, necessary that the irritation thus occasioned should be removed, and the removal could only be affected by fairness and conciliation, accompanied with personal intercourse and mutual explanation. In his effort to accomplish what was obviously just Sir Charles Bagot exactly carried into practice Mr. Baldwin's principle of " responsible government." It is true His Excellency said nothing about the legislature being a parliament, or the form of government being parliamentary, but, when he chose as his chief advisers "men possessed of the confidence of the representatives of the people," he sought to graft, so to speak, and for the first time on a lower legislature, attributes and powers that were pre-eminently parliamentary.

But the introduction of this new system was at first attended with consequences so practically inconvenient and apparently unjust that the home authorities were taken aback, and suddenly driven to consult old books, to examine old papers, in order that they might recover the old way of doing colonial work. As a result of such research it is probable that Lord Metcalfe, with other duties, was charged with the work of restoring, if possible, the earlier and what was then supposed to be the fairer and less harassing method of rule. In performing what he had undertaken to accomplish, he, like his predecessor, Lord Sydenham, played with the phrase "responsible government," and no doubt found comfort in shewing in what way and to what extent the principle was inapplicable to a subordinate legislature. The shadowy view of the subject which His Excellency endeavoured to present must have made it impossible for Mr. Baldwin to recognize his own more perfect picture. The resemblance was lost in the contrast, for Lord Metcalfe's benevolent softly-clad republican was wholly unlike Mr. Baldwin's sturdy half-naked democrat. In point of fact, between the resolutions of the Legislative Assembly and Lord Metcalfe's interpretation of them, there flowed a sea of separation which no sophistry could fathom and no art could bridge. The weight of responsibility had not only been weakened but it been placed elsewhere than on those upon whom it was intended it should rest. Nevertheless the people of Upper Canada were not generally dissatisfied, for mere abstract questions of constitutional government were at that period but little studied and less cared for.

In candour it must also be admitted that there were in those days a large number of persons who much preferred Lord Metcalfe's to Mr. Baldwin's theory of colonial rule, for there was an element of fatherhood in it which touched the hearts of a good many people, even when it eluded their comprehension. The party of indifference is a tolerably large one in all communities, and it is one, moreover, that is more apt to receive than to make impressions. Personal considerations and

M

individual likings influence such persons much more than subtle principles of law, or nice dissertations on usage and custom. With all such persons Lord Metcalfe's character had more weight than his opinions; admiration of the former acted like a charm. It could scarcely have been otherwise, for, under the glamour of his goodness, men refused to see a fault and hence they ceased to criticize and declined to argue. It occasioned, therefore, no great surprise when the elections that followed the resignation of the Baldwin-Lafontaine administration were over that the victory lay with the Governor General. Unfortunately the issue became a personal one, for His Excellency's supporters in many instances were known as the Governor's candidates. Thus was it that parliamentary government received a check, and the blossoming hopes of its friends were for several years blighted. The triumph, no doubt, was a calamity, for it resulted in disappointment to the Governor, and misfortune to the country. It placed the former in an attitude, in which no Governor should be found, of personal hostility to one of the two great parties into which English-speaking communities are usually divided, and it encouraged people to talk of the " supporters " and " opponents " of His Excellency. The latter, in like manner, suffered loss. For at a very critical time, when political education was in its infancy and the amenities of party warfare had only began to be cultivated, the electorate was passionately disturbed by unfair and disquieting cries which obscured or withdrew attention from the question at issue and encouraged people to resort to acts of violence ; and thus to settle by force questions that might perhaps have been easily quieted by reason.

But, if a restless policy obtained in Canada, a somewhat uncertain one ruled at Downing street. We have noticed Lord John Russell's instructions to Lord Sydenham on the subject of responsible government, and we may fairly conjecture that those of his successor, Lord Stanley, were not less direct and emphatic. Indeed we may do so without much risk of falling into error, for the compliments which Lord Metcalfe received from the Colonial Secretary on his retirement from the service would have been pure irony had they not meant that, in the opinion of the Government, he had faithfully carried out his instructions, and had scrupulously discharged his duty. Letters and despatches cannot always be printed with advantage. Lord Metcalfe's biographer has not, we think, in this respect shown discretion in his memoir of that nobleman, for many of the letters were evidently confidential and ought not to have been printed. Perhaps for the same reason it might be inexpedient to make public the despatches that were written by the " fiery Tybalt," the " Rupert of debate," as the late Earl of Derby, when a member of the House of Commons, was sometimes called. As Colonial Secretary that impetuous statesman had in all probability to send instructions to Sir Charles Bagot

and also to Lord Metcalfe on very delicate subjects;
what those instructions were we know not, but they
could scarcely have been expressed in the same words.
The policy of Sir Charles Bagot had no doubt occasioned
disquiet, and he was probably warned and recommended
to observe caution. The policy of Lord Metcalfe, though
not in harmony with the newly adopted views on
colonial administration, was of a character which had
been approved by experience and by Downing street
traditions, and therefore, as we venture to think, the
words of recognition were pointed with encouragement, and more, and made emphatic with honours,
for they were supplemented with a coronet. A
review of those passages of our history by such a
critic as the late Earl of Derby would no doubt be
pleasant reading to all, especially to those who can
remember not only the political drama, but the social
characteristics of the period. The tangle of public and private life was frequently amusing and sometimes instructive, for the wear and fret which interrupted
the former, though inconsistent with, was accompanied
by the mirth and fun that brightened the latter. If
men in these days fought more and reflected less, they,
at all events, were more mirthful than their successors,
and had the knack of making pleasantry contagious.
But other qualities than social ones were needed. The
state of parties in those days of irritation made the
work of government always difficult, and occasionally

impossible, while the suggested modes of escape from sudden entanglements showed how far people had drifted from safe ideas of administration. The Draper-Caron-Lafontaine correspondence is still an amusing piece of reading. The subtle art with which Mr. Draper, like the spider in the fable, sought to tempt Mr. Caron into his parlour was sufficiently clever, but it failed of its purpose. Whether it produced any effect on Mr. Caron's mind is uncertain, but it did not beguile Mr. Lafontaine and his friends to break their ranks or weaken their power by dividing it. On the last-named gentleman Mr. Draper's coaxing ways were alike importunate and vain, for they neither impressed the imagination nor influenced the conduct of those whom they were designed to reach. Mr. Lafontaine, moreover, had stated reasons for standing aloof, as he had mature opinions not only on what the government should be, but also on the position which his countrymen of French origin should fill in the government. For the purposes of administration the re-united province was according to his plan to be again separated, as it was his desire to rule by a double ministry in the same cabinet, and a double majority in the same legislature. Mr. Baldwin's idea, on the contrary, was administrative unity, irrespective of sectional majorities; and his there can be no doubt was the more convenient and practical view. Representatives of localities we may be quite sure will always look after their sectional interests, and hence no obliga-

tions to do so need be exacted. Nevertheless their
general conduct and procedure are expected to be controlled by influences held in subordination to their
higher duties as representatives of the whole people.
For they are trustees for the commonwealth, and not delegates of sections or caretakers of localities.

But just as those gentlemen had reached a serious
point in their literary skirmishing, and it was prolonged
for about ten months, Lord Metcalfe's illness obliged
him to resign and to go home. His Excellency's departure brought the Draper-Caron-Lafontaine correspondence to a sudden and uncomfortable close, for it not
only ended in reproaches and recrimination, but it
left the political issues of the country in a state of
more hopeless antagonism than ever. Government
became more and more difficult, and in this condition
it was found when Lord Elgin was welcomed as Gov-
ernor-General on the 30th January, 1847. His Excellency's arrival and the succession of Earl Grey to
the office of Secretary of State for the Colonies represent an important epoch in the history of the British
Colonies, and they suggest some reflections that are
pertinent to the study and review in which we are
engaged.

As in the matter of parliamentary privileges the
British Government seems to have been silent, or, if it
had spoken at all, the tones were so muffled as to escape the ears of those whom they chiefly interested, so

also in the matter of responsible or constitutional government, Colonial secretaries for the most part had only quoted the phrase to scout the principle it represented, while the two Houses of the Imperial Parliament had spoken with one voice to warn all whom it might concern, to have nothing whatever to do with it. But the teachings of seven years, though they wrought no change in the action of the Parliament, were not without effect on the opinion of the people of the United Kingdom. We know in what words Lord John Russell instructed Lord Sydenham in 1839, and, in the absence of exact information, we may be tolerably sure that Lord Stanley's directions to Sir Charles Bagot, as well as to Lord Metcalfe, were not less exact and emphatic, for the whigs and tories of those days generally held common sentiments on the way in which the government of the colonies should be administered.

It was, however, about the year 1839, and partly in consequence of the break down of the system of colonial rule in the two Canadas, that the teachings of the new school of colonial reformers began to influence public opinion. Men were constrained to bestow more attention on such subjects than they had done theretofore. Earl Grey was among the early converts to the theory of constitutional government, and Lord Elgin was perhaps the earliest Governor who fairly and frankly put the theory into practice. In 1846, Earl Grey, apparently regardless of the unanimous resolves of the Imperial Parliament, and of the instructions of his immediate predecessors in office, conceded, under another name, all that Mr. Baldwin had asked for, or had hoped to obtain. The instrument in which the conveyance is to be looked for is sufficiently imperfect, and appears to have no legal value, for it rests, so far as Canada is concerned, on the resolutions of one estate of the Legislature, and, so far as the mother country is concerned, on a conversation between Lord Grey and Lord Elgin. Still the resolutions and the conversation became vivified and hardened by the use to which they were put, and perhaps in these results have been found as real, and in many respects more operative, than some other measures that have received all the force that law can give them. Whatever the advantages may have been, and few will deny their importance, they seem to have reached us more by chance than by law, for they have been appropriated by the Canadian, rather than granted by the Imperial, legislature. Until the passing of the British North America Act, 1867, a ready answer could scarcely have been given to the question : "by what authority do ye these things, and who gave you this authority ? " So far as the British Government is concerned, the authority rests on the fluctuating opinions, nominally, of successive administrations, but practically of successive Colonial Secretaries, who, as we have seen, in the short space of seven years, promulgated three sets of conflicting, and in two instances of contradictory, instructions. So, also, it

was within the competency of a fourth or a fifth Colonial
Secretary to make further changes in the mode of administration, though it was beyond their power to make any
alteration in the law. Of the latter, the Parliament of the
United Kingdom, as we venture to think, was alike the
custodian and the interpreter.

No doubt the first governors of Upper and Lower
Canada acted under instructions, but there is reason to
think that such instructions were general, rather than
exact, in their terms. The constitutional act was to be
administered, but the way in which it was to be done, as
well as the ceremonials that were to accompany it, were
matters on which, so far as we have been able to discover, no orders were issued, and on which we may
therefore conclude that a liberal exercise of judgment was
permissible. Having to use a large discretion, Governor Simcoe, no doubt, desired to use it consistently. To
perfect the constitutional model he had set up in his
mind it was necessary to assume, and it was not difficult
to do so, that legislatures were parliaments, and, having
gone thus far in constructive analogy, it was quite natural to go a step farther, and in like manner to assume
that, being parliaments, they were also courts, and, being
courts, they ought to receive the consideration that is due
to the highest tribunals, especially when such courts are
periodically used as palaces wherein the representative
of majesty officially presides. Thus it came about
that the provincial legislatures, before and since the

confederation of the provinces, apparently assumed that
their Upper House of Assembly or their only House of
Assembly was and is a court, to be furnished with a
throne, and to be manned with apparators of different
ranks, including dignitaries of such stateliness as
ushers, and sergeants with emblems suggestive of royal
grace, such as black rods and gilt maces, swords,
lace, buckles, embroidery and collars of gold. Imitation is probably the sincerest form of flattery; and
it was due to the intensity of their desire to preserve and
perpetuate in the new provinces the customs of the
mother country that the founders of our usages took what
pains they could to preserve in miniature as fair a copy
as possible of those official ceremonials which some of
them had seen, and which all of them wished to cherish.
That provincial legislatures were not intended to be
parliaments, but only common councils of an earlier
pattern, was a view that seems not to have been taken
by any one. On the contrary, it was generally believed
in the past, and it is by no means wholly discredited at
the present time, notwithstanding the light which
Imperial laws have shed on the subject, that the terms
are convertible, and that the powers, privileges and
immunities that are distinctly conferred on parliaments
may be seized and appropriated, if they cannot otherwise be obtained, by legislatures. The old, and so far as
Canada is concerned, the hereditary, habit of thought,
survives Imperial corrections, for there are many per-

sons who, with ludicrous fidelity, and almost fanatic faith, still cling to what must be regarded as an erroneous, as well as an exploded rendering of words. No doubt the crown, if it imposed no restraint on its representatives in matters ceremonial, did much towards encouraging them to assume the functions and imitate the style of their sovereign. To this cause it may probably be attributed that the furnishings of the upper house of their Assembly included a throne ; and although the governors were powerless to bestow orders or confer distinctions, yet they thought themselves qualified to appoint officers whose titles in the mother country were and are inseparably associated with the blue ribband of English knighthood and the highest court of the United Kingdom, viz., the Order of the Garter and the High Court of Parliament. The conceit was, no doubt, very popular, and few suspected that it was also misleading. Indeed had not the delusion been disturbed and shattered by the Parliament of the United Kingdom, the simple faith of generations that have passed away would have remained unchallenged and unbroken. Nevertheless, had patience in the form of doubt stood on the threshold of our political existence, had a cold-blooded metaphysician and a severe economist, instead of a warm-hearted enthusiast and a natural poet, been appointed the first governor of Upper Canada, then the question which has given rise to this review would have been examined, and no doubt with disappointing

results.   A   pause   certainly   would   have   followed,
and, perhaps, an answer might have been given that,
among other direct and indirect consequences, would
have shut out from our view the military pageant, the
vice-regal presence, and the imposing ceremony of opening our provincial legislatures, together with the picturesque accessories that wait on that event.   Had the
question been patiently thought out when the Legislature
of Upper Canada began its modest career at Newark,
then we fear that three generations of Canadians would
never have heard the dialogue between the two speakers
at the beginning of a Parliament, and would never have
seen the ceremonial at the opening of each session,
where successive Black Rods have indulged in picturesque pantomimes in the upper house, and taken a
bold attitude of command in the lower one ; the double
duty having been gaily assumed on the strength of their
remote connection with a grand chapter of knighthood,
and their direct contact with a High Court of Parliament.
The day of humiliation and disappointment, happily for
them, was far off, and they passed away without being
aware of what we must regard as the fact that, as there
was neither a grand chapter of knighthood nor a high
Court of Parliament in Canada, they represented neither
the one nor the other, and therefore their office only
commenced in its true dignity when the Parliament of
Canada was created under the authority of the British
North America Act, 1867.

However, these superfluous ceremonies did not exactly express labour lost, but only labour exegetical if not misapplied, for there are analogies between things that are not the same. The legislatures of the Provinces thus became schools of instruction, and black rods and gold maces were assiduously doing their parts as educators of the state. Men learned in what way they ought to acquit themselves in matters of secular ritual, and so when the time arrived for them to possess in its fulness what they had theretofore seen only dimly and in shadow, they were quite prepared to recognize the distinctions that had been drawn for them, and to appreciate the exchange of a legislature for a parliament. And such knowledge was being acquired under the most favourable conditions. The public men of the period believed that they were required to do as they had done, for they thought substantial verities were expressed, as in truth they are, in ceremonies and formulas. The Parliament of the United Kingdom had given them constitutions, and had left to them the duty of working them out. It had not gone out of its way to instruct or to control them. It did not humble them with an imposition of superior knowledge, or make their darkness visible by shedding over it a flood of legal light. That ordeal was reserved for 1867, when they were to learn by a process of very emphatic and direct teaching, not only that legislatures were not parliaments, but that, like corporations of less pretence, their authorities and powers were limited by the terms of the statute under which they were created.

We are quite aware of the fact that in times past, and before 1867, very interesting questions on the jurisdiction of local legislatures were from time to time submitted to the courts. Without saying a word on the judgments rendered in those cases, for it would be unbecoming in us to do so, we may perhaps be excused for remarking that the judges had not then the advantage of seeing the interpretation which the Parliament of the United Kingdom, by the British North America Act, 1867, has impliedly, and by retrospect, put on the constitutional acts of 1791 and 1840. Had the fact been otherwise it is probable that some doubts would have been removed, possibly some opinions would have been qualified and others might have been changed. Judges might peradventure have said that, as the legislatures of Canada are not parliaments, we are not required to express any opinion on the subject, much less to transfer to the former privileges and powers that belong only to the latter. Parliament derives its authority from ancient custom or established usage, and not only from law. Legislatures, on the other hand, rest on a written basis which is plainly set forth in the Imperial statutes. Some such difficulty must, we think, have been present to the mind of the late Chief Justice Sir John B. Robinson, one of whose earlier judgments bears directly on the question under review. It was delivered about half a century ago, and will be found in " Draper's King's Bench Reports of Upper Canada." The action was one of trespass and false imprisonment brought by the late Sir Allan N. MacNab against Messieurs Bidwell and Baldwin, members of the House of Assembly, the former being the Speaker.

The defence was that the House of Assembly had a constitutional right to call persons before it for the purpose of obtaining information ; and, if the house adjudged the conduct of such persons in answering or in refusing to answer before a select committee to be a contempt, the house has the right to imprison them for such contempt.

Sir Allan N. MacNab having committed a contempt within the meaning of the above words was arrested on the Speaker's warrant, and imprisoned during the pleasure of the house from the 16th of February to the 3rd March. Hence the action.

In giving judgment the Chief Justice took exception to the exemplification of the case and administered a reproof to those who had drawn it up because they had used the word " Parliament " instead of " Legislature," as it was " technically wrong for any local legislature to assume other " designations than those assigned to it by the British statutes." It would have been more proper, the Chief Justice added, " to have preserved the precise names assigned to our legislature and its several branches in our written constitution." Having pointed out the

" inaccuracy which had better have been avoided," his lordship delivered an elaborate judgment, which, however, was entirely adverse to the pretentions of the plaintiff. But it is worthy of note that, while the Chief Justice deprecated the interchange of terms as "an inaccuracy which had better have been avoided," his judgment, nevertheless, seemed to rest on the idea that the names were interchangeable, for it pointed directly to the assumed analogy between the powers and privileges of the local legislature and those of the Imperial Parliament, adding, by way of zest, to his argument " that the absence of such powers would reduce the legislature to an utterly helpless and contemptible condition." Judge Sherwood, following and concurring with the Chief Justice, added " that the authority to make laws included the duty of making inquiry, and this duty implies a right to compel the persons examined to answer all lawful questions." The Judge did not pause to inquire whether a House of Assembly was a court, and, if not, whence came the power to compel. The difficulty, though in another aspect, did not escape the Chief Justice, who observed, " that the authority of the House of Commons to commit has, when questioned, been sustained by the courts upon the grounds of precedent and usage only." This view seems to have represented a difficulty, and, at the same time, to have suggested a way of escaping from it, for the Chief Justice continued: "it is material to consider that this usage must have had a beginning, and that, in the first instance, we must suppose the power to have been assumed and acquiesced in from a conviction that, upon principle, it might and ought to be exercised." Of course usage, or the necessity for it, precedes law, " as nothing can come into an Act of Parliament but it must be first affirmed or propounded by somebody." But the difficulty thus admitted is suggestive. Whether the mode of escape thus indicated is the only one, is a question to which a very thoughtful answer should be given.

The analogies which the Chief Justice described as existing between the powers and duties of the legislatures and those of the Imperial Parliament were then supposed to be absolutely correct. No one at that time imagined they rested on different, if not opposite, foundations. Of course they were regarded as applicable by Governor Simcoe, for he was the first to institute such analogies. They were naturally accepted and easily transmitted, and would, in all probability, be now received as true and well established had they not been virtually controverted, if not absolutely destroyed, by the British North America Act 1867.

Nor should it be overlooked that, while the two Canadian provinces appear to have arrived at a thorough agreement on the way in which certain things ought to be done and on the words in which such doings should be expressed, the other provinces in British North America seem to have adopted a form which apparently was derived from the older province of Nova

N

Scotia though we do not know how it came to be introduced there. For example, in the two Canadas all the
proceedings of the Legislature ran in the name of the
Sovereign. Every law was " enacted by the King's (or
Queen's) Most Excellent Majesty by and with the advice
and consent of the Legislative Council and Assembly
of the Province." In like manner, when laws were
assented to, the assent was given in the name of the
Sovereign, thus " in His (or Her) Majesty's name His
Excellency the Governor General, or Lieutenant-Governor assents to this Bill." In Nova Scotia and New
Brunswick the enacting clause of the laws ran thus:
" Be it enacted by the Lieutenant-Governor, Legislative Council and Assembly as follows." In like
manner the laws received the personal assent of
the Lieutenant-Governors in the words " I assent to
this bill." But when bills were reserved they were so
reserved for the " signification of Her Majesty's pleasure." It may also be remarked that Governor Simcoe
in the first session of the Upper Canada Legislature,
gave his personal assent to bills without using the name,
or authority, of His Majesty. In the next session the
form was changed to " His Majesty's name." The Prince
Edward Island form ought not to be overlooked, for it
includes a distinction that has been somewhat lost sight of.
Before the confederation of the provinces, when the island
was an immediate dependency of the Crown, the assent to
bills was given in the Queen's name. Since the island has

become a province of the Dominion, and consequently one of the legislative planets, that revolve round the central Parliament of Canada, the form has, we think, been properly adapted to the new system, for the Lieutenant Governor personally assents to Bills. In the province of British Columbia, curiously enough, the matter is reversed, and the change is all the other way. When that province was directly connected with Great Britain the laws were enacted by the Governor by and with the advice and consent of the Legislative Council, while since Confederation " Her Majesty " is substituted for the Governor. These varieties of formula shew that the new page in Canadian history has been differently understood by different readers, and, consequently, a large crop of doubts, accompanied with some perplexities and many disappointments, has steadily grown up. Authority has been unduly warped and misapplied, for the legislatures have steadily sought to appropriate privileges and powers that were conferred on parliament alone. It, therefore, became a duty to restrain vaulting ambition and to rebuke local assumption. It was necessary to refer provincial statesmen to the indentures under which they had taken service, and to tell them politely that the difference between a legislature and a parliament is a very real and a very wide one, and that the former was never meant to be the counterpart of the latter. The idea of the two words meaning the same thing evidently was as absent from the mind, as the intention was from the act of the mother country.

Since the earlier part of this review was written some interesting questions have arisen that will probably lead to important statements that may remove doubts on the relations that should subsist between the Parliament of Canada and the legislatures of the respective provinces. Without hazarding a conjecture as to the nature of those statements we may, at all events, assume that one disputed point will be set quietly at rest. Dr. Baldwin's contention in 1812 on the subject of privileges will probably be reconsidered, and the local legislatures will be left exactly in the situation in which they were intended to be placed by the law makers, and were placed by the law. The fallacy that legislatures cannot be distinguished from parliaments will disappear, for few will be found of sufficient hardihood to assert that two organizations with different titles and unequal powers may properly be described as identical organizations with the advantage of having interchangeable names.

The twelfth section of the British North America Act, 1877, reads as follows :

All Powers, Authorities, and Functions which, under any Act of the Parliament of Great Britain, or of the Parliament of the United Kingdom of Great Britain and Ireland, or of the Legislature of Upper Canada, Lower Canada, Canada, Nova Scotia, or New-Brunswick, are, at the Union, vested in or exerciseable by the respective Governors or Lieutenant Governors of those Provinces, with the advice, or with the advice and consent, of the respective Executive Councils thereof, or in conjunction with those Councils, or with any number of members thereof, or by those Governors or

Lieutenant Governors individually, shall, as far as the same continue in existence and capable of being exercised after the Union,
in relation to the Government of Canada, be vested in and exerciseable by the Governor General, with the advice, or with the advice and consent of, or in conjunction with the Queen's Privy
Council for Canada, or any members thereof, or by the Governor
General individually, as the case requires, subject, nevertheless,
(except with respect to such as exist under Acts of the Parliament
of Great Britain or of the Parliament of the United Kingdom of
Great Britain and Ireland) to be abolished or altered by the Parliament of Canada."

It will be observed that the hinge on which all authority is made to turn is law.   It may be colonial law or it
may be imperial law, but it must be law.   Usage, custom, resolutions, conversations, despatches, instructions,
have no place in the clause.   Being absent, such conditions or qualifications must, we apprehend, be regarded
as excluded, and, consequently, of little value when we
search for the legal meanings of plain words.   If by their
written constitutions the local legislatures are shut out
from the advantages which parliaments derive from
custom and usage, then the law alone must be their directory, for they are not at liberty to go elsewhere for
guidance. The conclusion, therefore, seems to be that they
may use any powers or privileges that are given to them
by law, but that they have no right to use what they
take without leave.   No doubt such results as these, if
they are well founded and fairly arrived at, would carry
with them some disappointing, as well as some desirable

consequences. Among the latter, and by no means the least important, is the relative status of legislatures as compared with parliaments, and by how many well drawn lines of distinction they are separated one from the other.

The British North America Act 1867, under the head of the distribution of legislative powers, sheds further light on the subject of this inquiry. For example, certain special matters are assigned to the absolute control of the Parliament of Canada, while other matters equally special are assigned to the absolute control of the legislatures of the provinces. There appears, however, to be a suggestive proviso in respect to un-enumerated subjects which is worthy of note, for it has already given rise to differences of opinion as well as an interesting correspondence between the local and federal governments. The United States constitution provides that "the powers not delegated to the United States by the constitution, nor prohibited by it to the states, are reserved to the states respectively," while the constitution of Canada seems to reverse this procedure, for it includes in the powers of parliament "all matters not coming within the classes of subjects by this act assigned exclusively to the legislatures of the provinces." In the former case the separate states appear to receive the benefit of the doubt, while in the latter the benefit adheres to the federal government. Since public bodies, like private individuals, do not generally desire to court a diminution of power, it is probable that this, among

other questions that may have seemed tolerably clear to
the authors of the British North America Act, will
eventually be relegated to some disinterested and impartial tribunal, either in Canada or in the mother country.
In the meanwhile, and until the practice is reversed by
authority, we may conclude that whatever powers were
not expressly given to the provinces will be looked
upon as trusts to be administered for the whole people
by the Parliament of Canada.

It should also be borne in mind that the provincial
legislatures which were created by the Act of 1867 are
not equal in power and authority to the legislatures
whose places they have taken. This must obviously be
the case, for the authority within their municipal limits,
which the former legislatures exercised, was in several
important particulars transferred to the Parliament of
Canada. The reflection naturally arises, if those legislatures were not parliaments in the halcyon days of their
existence, much less are their successors parliaments
now, for they lack several of the conditions which shed
a pleasing, but delusive, glamour over the earlier period.
The governors of provinces, for example, are no longer
officers appointed directly by the Crown, but only a part
of the administrative staff of the Parliament of Canada.
The Governor General being the representative of the
crown, absorbs in his own person the delegated
attributes of the crown, and intercepts, so to speak, the
direct current of prerogative. This function of prero-

gative was given to him to administer, and to him alone, and we doubt if he has the power to delegate it to another. In a despatch to the Governor General of the 7th January, 1875, Lord Carnarvon said : " They, the Lieutenant Governors of the Provinces of the Dominion, however important locally their functions may be, are a part of the colonial administrative staff, and are more immediately responsible to the Governor General in Council. They do not hold commissions from the crown, and neither in power nor privilege resemble those governors of colonies to whom, after special consideration of their personal fitness, the Queen, under the great seal and her own hand and signet, delegates portions of her prerogatives and issues her own instructions."

If Lieutenant Governors are not officers of the Crown, we naturally inquire in what degree they stand related to the representative of the Crown. Are they not the Deputies, in their respective provinces, of the Governor General of Canada ? They receive their appointments, under the advice of the Privy Council, from His Excellency, and they hold their appointments, under certain conditions, during the pleasure of His Excellency.

The difference which at first sight may appear sentimental becomes very real as we examine it more closely, for it not only touches the executive, but it disturbs the legislative authority. Not only does there exist a great difference between the powers of a parliament on one hand, and a legislature on the other, but the distinction is broader and more strongly marked when we examine the component parts of those bodies.

In a report of a Committee of the Honourable the Privy Council, approved by His Excellency the Governor General in Council on the 1st of April, 1875, the committee advised that an act passed by the Legislature of Ontario, intituled " An Act respecting Escheats and Forfeitures," should be disallowed. The reasons for the advice include an elaborate argument of the then Minister of Justice, Mr. Fournier, from which a few suggestive extracts may be made. It is true that the argument did not turn out to be conclusive, for it was, as we understand it, subsequently set aside on the ground that it failed to embrace considerations that existed before, and that were not invalidated by, the passage of the British North America Act, 1867. Apart, however, from the issues of fact and of law thus raised, on which it would be highly presumptuous for us to offer any remark, we may take advantage of Mr. Fournier's observations on the question that is more immediately under consideration. Mr. Fournier, in speaking of the relative authority of the parliament and of the legislatures, took occasion to observe that under the British North America Act, 1867, the Parliament of Canada is defined to consist of the Queen, the Senate and the House of Commons, and the mode of legislation by parliament is defined to be that of the Queen, by and with the advice of the Senate and House of Commons.

On the other hand, the legislature of each province
has a different definition. Take that of Ontario, for
example. It is found to consist of the Lieutenant Governor, and of one house styled " the Legislative Assembly
of Ontario." In continuation, Mr. Fournier says : " It
is true that the legislatures of the different provinces, in
enacting laws, have used the terms : ' Her Majesty, by
and with the advice of and consent of the Legislative
Council and Assembly of the Province ' (or, in respect of
Ontario, of the Legislative Assembly of Ontario alone),
and it may have been thought expedient to adopt that
formula ; yet little doubt can be entertained that the
same is incorrect, and that the enacting party should be,
under section 92, ' The Legislature' of the Province."
" A Lieutenant Governor" (not having been appointed
by the Queen) "has no power," Mr. Fournier says, " to
assent to any laws of a legislature in the Queen's name,
inasmuch as the Queen herself has not that power, and
cannot therefore depute it."

" The only instance in which," to the knowledge of Mr.
Fournier, " there is an express delegation to a Lieutenant
Governor of privileges of the Crown is in the commission
of the Governor General, the sixth section of which is thus
worded : ' And we do further authorize and empower you
to exercise, from time to time as you may judge necessary, all powers lawfully belonging to us, in respect of
assembling or proroguing the Senate or the House of
Commons of our said Dominion, and of dissolving the

said House of Commons, and we do hereby give the like authority to the several Lieutenant Governors for the time being of the provinces of our said Dominion with respect to the Legislative Councils or the legislative or general assemblies of those provinces respectively."

On this passage we do not propose to dwell, for, as we have elsewhere remarked, it seems by the different formulas that have been adopted, to have been differently understood by the authorities in the different provinces.

Mr. Fournier continues to observe that the foregoing allusions and others that we have not extracted " are made as supporting the view already expressed, that the Parliament of Canada, to which " the Queen is an actual party by name and the actual enacting power, by and with the advice and consent of the two Houses of Parliament, is the only legislative power which can operate in matters not left to the provincial legislatures ; and that the Queen, not being in any way an enacting party, or power of such a Legislature, Her Majesty's name is improperly used in provincial legislation."

The Lieutenant Governor of a Province, next to the Governor General of Canada, fills one of the most responsible situations in the Dominion. It is more than imposing, and requires no doubtful bracing for its support and no borrowed burnishing to make it shine. Plain and unadorned the two words " Lieutenant Governor " convey no doubtful meaning, for they are alike suggestive of simplicity and strength ; moreover, they have a sterling ring about them whose tone could not be improved by any amount of borrowed plating.   There are, however, graver reasons why this process of embellishment should be avoided. Shams of all sorts are generally distrusted, and are to be looked upon with suspicion, but shams in high places are especially to be condemned, for they provoke imitation in low ones, and excuse, if they do not give rise, to pretence and imposture.

But while governors have displayed a lack of subordination by consenting to assume distinctive titles that belong only to the Governor General, so also have the legislatures become insubordinate by attempting to seize powers that belong only to the Parliament of Canada.   The latter have seemed to resent, so to speak, the state of political life in which they were placed by the mother country.   With the natural aspirations of ordinary people they have striven to become more than they were intended to be, and with concerted energy have endeavoured to lift themselves to a higher plane in the political orbit.   Reasoning from analogy, they may have thought that as Lieutenant Governors had adopted, and apparently had retained, the distinctive title of " Excellency " without any audible expression of dissent having been heard, so also might provincial legislatures appropriate the name of " Parliaments " without any fear of either criticism or rebuke.   There was, however, a difference in the two transactions. Both were irregularities, and in different degrees were breaches of courtesy, but neither lacked the support of arguments that were wholly fallacious. The discourtesy in the case of Lieutenant Governors was qualified by the creditable desire it displayed to connect their office directly, rather than intermediately, with the supreme authority, for they, no doubt, wished to be accounted representatives of Her Majesty. The offence of the local legislatures was of the like character, but it included consequences of more serious importance. If not actually envious of the "Parliament of Canada," the legislatures did what people sometimes do who are overcome with the spirit of covetousness. They desired to possess themselves of the like privileges, immunities and powers to those which had exclusively been granted to the Parliament of Canada. Instead, however, of applying to the source whence the Parliament of Canada received such exceptional advantages, they sought, by the adoption of a unique expedient, to confer them on themselves. By a vote of their own, which was formally hardened into an act of their own, they determined, by and with the advice of the Queen's Most Excellent Majesty, and irrespective of the Parliament of the United Kingdom, to confer on themselves the like privileges which that Parliament had exclusively bestowed on the "Senate and House of Commons of Canada, and on the Members thereof."

For the sake of convenience we shall follow the course
of the narrative from whence our information is derived,
rather than the chronological arrangement which at first
sight might appear more convenient. In a despatch
addressed to the Minister of Justice the Lieutenant
Governor of Manitoba, in the year 1874, complained that
a bill intituled "an Act defining the privileges and immunities of the Legislative Council and Assembly of
Manitoba," to which he had given his assent, had been
disallowed. The Lieutenant Governor naturally thought
that act was within the competency of the legislature
of his government, because the legislatures of Ontario,
Quebec and British Columbia had passed acts of a
similar character, all of which had been left to their
operation. This conclusion was only true in part, for
those acts were looked upon as so important and unusual that the authorities at Ottawa, and notably the
Minister of Justice, adopted the wise and safe course of
referring two of them to the Colonial Secretary, in order
that they might be submitted to the Law Officers of the
Crown for their opinion. In the course of time the
opinion sought for was received, and it was found to be
entirely adverse to the provincial legislatures and to the
acts which they had respectively passed. Those acts were
ultra vires, and in excess of the powers which the local
legislatures had received. Consequently, the Ontario
and Quebec acts were disallowed, while the act of the
Legislature of British Columbia was repealed in the
same session in which it was introduced.

This episode in the history of provincial legislatures is alike suggestive and instructing. The discrimination made by the British America Act 1867 between "legislatures" and "parliaments" was not an idle one, having only a verbal value. On the contrary it drew broad distinctions and carried real meanings, whose importance can scarcely be exaggerated. The Parliament of Canada had been made the recipient of honours and trusts that had not only been withheld from the legislatures of the Provinces, but which had not, till then, been conferred on any of the colonies. The legislatures, no doubt, desired to become possessed of the privileges and advantages which had been conferred on the Parliament of Canada. And the question arose as to how they might be acquired. They could not, as in the earlier days, be appropriated as a matter of course, as if they were integral parts of Governor Simcoe's image and transcript of the British constitution. The British North America Act of 1867 had placed such a proceeding beyond reach. What was to be done? As authority could not be taken either under the sanction of custom, usage or Imperial law might it not be acquired under the sanction and protection of colonial statutes. The effort was made in four provinces. The acts of two legislatures of the larger of those provinces were submitted to the law officers of the Crown, with what result we have already seen. Their rendering reads like a verdict, and it seems to echo

Dr. Baldwin's contention, expressed more than sixty years earlier.

There is another parallel, for even in this question of privilege history repeats itself. In his judgment in the case of MacNab *vs.* Bidwell and Baldwin, the late Chief Justice, Sir John Robinson, took occasion to rebuke the parties to the suit for inexactness in the use of terms, and for styling the Upper Canada legislature a parliament and the legislative assembly a house of commons, so in like manner, but forty-six years later, exception is taken by the Minister of Justice, Mr. Blake, for the like inexactness to that for which the old legislature of Upper Canada had been reproved. When reporting on an act intituled " An Act respecting the election of members of the Legislative Assembly of the Province of Quebec," Mr. Blake took exception to the phrases " parliamentary electors " and " holding of parliamentary elections " and calls the attention of the Lieutenant Governor to such irregularities. The like objections were also taken to a similar act passed by the Legislature of Manitoba. Inexactness leads to confusion. Had the early governments of the different provinces been careful in their official formulas to use for descriptive purposes the language only of the acts under which their legislatures were constituted, there would have been no justification for Dr. Baldwin's contention in 1812, and probably no excuse in 1879 for this

STUDY AND REVIEW.

www.ingramcontent.com/pod-product-compliance
Lightning Source LLC
Chambersburg PA
CBHW030827270326
41928CB00007B/926